POLISH
YOUR KITCHEN

MY FAMILY TABLE

by ANNA HURNING

– Table of contents –

Desserts

Index

Acknowledgements

For Hanna,

*so you never have to search
for where you came from.*

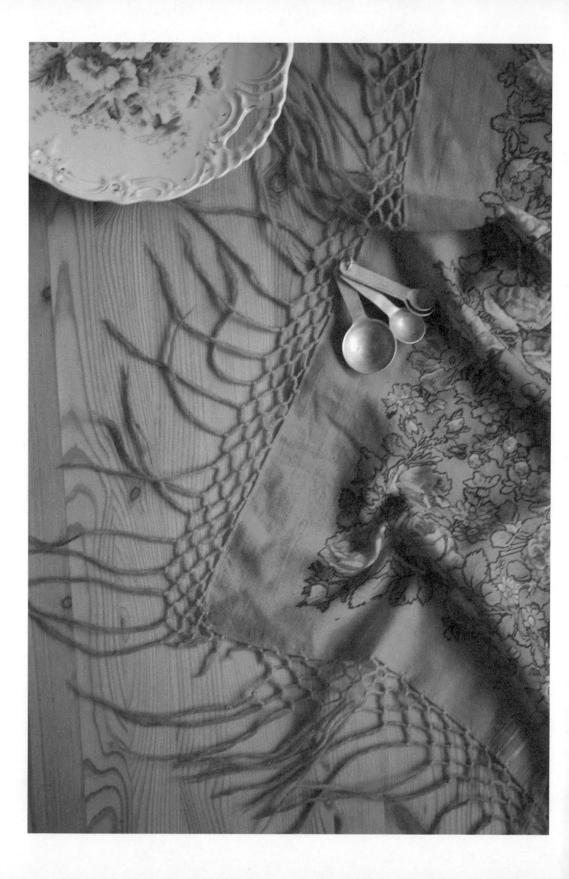

— Introduction —

This is my family table. It's a bit old; it has scratches and stains from family gatherings and early mornings when my daughter was little. You can see indentations of writing from when she was doing her homework as she got a little older. You can see cracks in the legs from when it was moved seven times during our life together. It carries our memories, family traditions, and secrets, and it represents our family going back four generations.

The red, flowery scarf belonged to my great-grandmother Józefa. I didn't know her. She was born and raised in a small village outside Sieradz, Poland. She passed away when my grandma was little, during WWII. I don't even know what she looked like, as there are no surviving photographs of her. The red scarf is the only material thing that is left from her. She, unknowingly, sits at our table. It's her recipes and the recipes passed down by her sisters that are being served here. Babcia Stasia, her daughter, sits here too. My whole knowledge of home cooking comes from her. It's the flavors that she produced that make me emotional and nostalgic. Her cooking is comfort food.

After moving from Poland to the US, away from my home town of Szczecin and my Polish family, I've developed my own style of cooking combing knowledge from both sides of my family. My paternal grandma, babcia Władzia, was an excellent home chef as well. She was the master of making something out of nothing. She was also very generous when ingredients were plenty. Her cooking looked so easy, even though she never took shortcuts and made everything from scratch. She is also present at our table.

This book represents influences of great-grandmothers, grandmothers, parents, and our take on traditional Polish recipes. It embodies the food of my family and dishes that are still prepared and served regularly. This book will allow my daughter to continue visiting with our ancestors at our table.

Pull up a chair and meet my family. This is my family table.

Anna Hurning

Soups

Zupy

Bean Soup

—Zupa fasolowa—

Thick and filling soup
prepared with smoked sausage and vegetables.

Yields: *9–10 servings*   **Prep time:** *10 minutes*   **Cook time:** *20 minutes*

4 oz / 120 g of smoked slab bacon (or a small smoked ham hock, a few smoked pork ribs, or a link of good quality smoked Polish sausage)

1 large onion, chopped

2 bay leaves

4–5 whole peppercorns and allspice berries (each)

1 tsp of salt

3 small carrots, peeled and sliced

2 c of diced potatoes

6 c / 1 ½ l of water

Two 15 oz / 425 g cans of northern beans (or other white beans)

½ c / 120 ml of cold water

2 tbsp of all-purpose flour

½ tbsp of dried marjoram

Place slab bacon in a medium pan and heat to release some grease. (If using ham hocks, place 2 tablesoons of butter in a medium pan instead to sauté the onion. Add ham hocks when adding water. If using smoked sausage, dice and sauté with onions.) Add onions and sauté for about 5 minutes.

Add bay leaves, peppercorns and allspice berries, salt, carrots, potatoes, and water. Drain and rinse beans and add to soup. Simmer on medium-low for about 15–20 minutes, until all veggies are soft.

To finish off the soup, whisk flour with cold water until well combined and add to hot soup. Bring to boil to thicken. Add marjoram, stir and taste. Add more salt, if needed.

Anna's note:

Let it rest a bit for flavors to combine (about 30–60 minutes).
Serve hot with a slice of hearty bread.

13

Anna's note:

Red barszcz loses it's color when boiled, this is why I recommend letting the soup sit overnight for flavors to combine. Limit boiling when reheating also. Vinegar will help with preserving the color.

Beetroot Vegetable Soup

— Barszcz ukraiński —

*Beef-based broth with earthy tones of beets
and aromatic vegetables.*

Yields: *10 servings*   **Prep time:** *15 minutes*   **Cook time:** *1.5 hours*

2 lbs / 1 kg / 6–7 small / medium beets

12–14 oz / 350–380 g beef soup bones or beef ribs

6 c / 1 ½ l of water

1 tsp of salt

2 carrots

¼ of an onion

5–6 whole peppercorns and allspice berries (each)

3 bay leaves

2 c / 8 oz / 240 g of fresh green beans

One 15.5 oz / 439 g can of white kidney beans

One 15.5 oz / 439 g can of navy beans

3–4 medium potatoes

3 c / 300 g / about ½ of a small head of fresh green cabbage

⅛ c of white vinegar

1 garlic clove, crushed

½ c of sweet cream

2 tbsp of all-purpose flour

Dill for garnish

Preheat oven to 350°F / 180°C. Cut stems off the beets (at the stem, not the bulb) and scrub them well under running water. Place in a baking dish, cover with aluminum foil and bake until soft (large ones will take 1.5 hours). Take out, cool, peel and grate on the largest vegetable grater—you may want to use gloves and protect your garments for this part.

While beets are baking, place beef bones in a large stockpot, add water, salt, peeled carrots, onion, allspice berries and peppercorns, and bay leaves. Cover and simmer for 1 hour. Remove carrots and set aside. Continue simmering for another 30 minutes.

In the meantime, wash fresh green beans, cut stem ends off and cut into about 1 inch / 3 centimeter pieces. Drain and rinse canned beans, set aside. Peel and cube potatoes (keep in cold water until ready to add to soup), set aside. Chop fresh cabbage, set aside.

After a total of 1 ½ hours of boiling beef broth, take out beef bones and add 2 cups / 500 milliliters of water. Next, add potatoes and green beans. Bring to boil and simmer for 10 minutes. Next, add canned beans, cabbage, and sliced carrots. Bring to boil and simmer for another 5 minutes.

At this time, turn heat off, add vinegar, shredded beets, and crushed garlic clove. I also added about ½ teaspoon of salt. Give it a stir and set aside for at least two hours (preferably overnight).

When ready to eat, mix sweet cream with flour and slowly add about 1 cup of soup to it to temper it. Stir well to combine. Add flour mixture to hot soup and heat until almost boiling. Taste and add a bit more salt, if needed.

Sprinkle with fresh dill and serve hot.

Cabbage & Sausage Soup

—Zupa z kapusty, z kiełbasą—

Light vegetable and cabbage broth with smoky sausage.

Yields: *6–8 servings*   **Prep time:** *10 minutes*   **Cook time:** *20–30 minutes*

12–16 oz / 350–500 g of good quality smoked sausage

1 onion, chopped

3 bay leaves

5–6 whole peppercorns and allspice berries (each)

8 c / 2 l of water or stock

1 c of carrots, sliced

1 parsnip or parsley root

3 celery stalks or ¼ of a celery root, diced

½ head of medium cabbage, chopped

One 14.5 oz / 400 g can of diced tomatoes or 4 fresh tomatoes or 3–4 tbsp of tomato paste

Salt to taste

Dice sausage and place in a soup pot. Sear until the edges are golden brown. Add chopped onion, bay leaves, peppercorns and allspice berries. Sauté until onion is cooked.

Add water / stock, carrots, parsnip, celery, and a bit of salt (amount will depend on whether you're using water or stock).

Simmer on low for about 15–20 minutes, or until vegetables are soft.

In the meantime, chop the cabbage. When stock is ready, add cabbage and tomatoes / tomato paste.

Boil for another 5–10 minutes, until cabbage softens. Do not overcook the cabbage. You want a bit of crunch in it.

Taste and add a bit more salt, if needed.

Anna's note:

Some cooks like to add potatoes; I sometimes do too. The amount of cabbage and sausage added may vary too. After you make it once or twice, you'll find the best way to suit your taste buds.

Chicken Soup

— Rosół —

Delicious, clear chicken broth cooked with vegetables and served with homemade noodles. "Rosół" is every Pole's favorite Sunday soup.

Yields: *8 servings*   **Prep time:** *10 minutes*   **Cook time:** *2 hours*

1 good quality whole chicken

2 carrots

1 parsley root (or parsnip)

¼–½ of a celery root

A few leaves of a leek (the dark green parts)

¼ of a large onion

4 bay leaves

6 whole peppercorns and all-spice berries (each)

1 tbsp of salt

A few sprigs of green parsley for garnish

Wash chicken and peel and wash vegetables. Place all (minus the onion) in a large pot. Fill with water to cover (about 2 quarts / 2 liters).

Place onion on the open flame of the burner and burn both sides of the cut quarter. If using an electric stove, place in a dry pan and heat until the onion burns on the surface. Add to the mix. Add bay leaves, peppercorns, allspice berries, and salt.

Cover the pot and bring to boil, then turn heat down and simmer on low for about 2 hours. We only want the water to lightly bubble.

After 2 hours and when chicken is tender and falls off the bone, remove and take off the bone.

Fill each serving bowl with a few scoops of boiled pasta (if using store-bought, I like the thin egg noodles or angel hair pasta), add a few slices of carrot, some meat (if you'd like) and garnish with a pinch of chopped parsley. Fill bowl with hot liquid and enjoy!

Recipe for homemade soup noodles on page 69!

Chilled Beetroot Soup

— Chłodnik —

*Cold beetroot soup full of fresh flavor
prepared in the summer.*

Yields: *3–4 servings*   **Prep time:** *10 mintes + up to 1 hour for roasting beets*

4 small beets (or 2 large)

4 radishes

3 tbsp of chopped dill

4 tbsp of chives

1–2 pickling cucumbers (or about ⅓ of an English cucumber)

1 small garlic clove

1 tbsp of white vinegar

A squeeze of lemon

2 c / 500 ml of buttermilk

½–1 c / 120–230 ml of plain yogurt

1 tsp of salt

1 tsp of sugar

3–4 hard-boiled eggs

Preheat oven to 350°F / 180°C. Wash beets and trim off the stems, but don't cut into the beet (we don't want the juices to flow out).

Roast in a roasting pan with a cover (or covered with tin foil) until soft (small beets about 30 minutes; large around 1 hour). Take out and cool completely. Once cool, peel and grate on the largest side of a box grater. Set aside.

Wash radishes and cut into thin slices. Chop dill and chives. Peel cucumber and dice.

Place all vegetables and herbs into a mixing bowl (or a pot) and add minced garlic, vinegar, lemon juice, buttermilk, and yogurt and stir. Also add salt and sugar.

Taste and add more salt, if needed. Soup should be relatively salty.

Chill well before serving. Serve with a hard-boiled egg.

Anna's note:

IMPORTANT: *some wild mushrooms are not to be served to children. Do your research before serving to children.*

Christmas Beetroot Broth with Mushroom Dumplings

— Barszcz wigilijny z uszkami —

Vegetarian beetrooot broth with tangy notes, served with wild-mushroom-filled soup dumplings. This soup is the star of every Polish Christmas Eve dinner table.

Yields: *6–7 servings*   **Prep time:** *5 days*   **Cook time:** *1 hour*

— Starter & Broth —

STARTER:

About 1 lb / ½ kg of fresh beets

1 tsp of sugar

1 tbsp of salt

4 garlic cloves, crushed

A piece of rye, pumpernickel or sourdough bread (if you have)

1 qt / 1 l of boiled and cooled water

ADDITIONALLY:

A pickling crock or glass jar

BROTH:

2 ½ c / 2 oz / 60 g of dried wild mushrooms*

2 ½ c / 600 ml of water

½ of a celery root or 1 celery stalk

2 carrots

1 parsnip

¼ of an onion burnt straight on a gas burner

6 whole peppercorns and all-spice berries (each)

½ tsp of salt

¼ c of vinegar (4%)

3 medium beets

1 tbsp of butter

Sprinkle of dried marjoram

3 garlic cloves, crushed

1 ½ tsp of sugar

Wash, peel and slice your beets into thin slices. Place in a sterilized glass or ceramic pickling container. Add sugar, salt, garlic, bread, and water. Set on the counter for 5 days to sour.

One night before you're ready to cook broth, place dried mushrooms in a pot and add 2 ½ cups of water to soak (make sure the pot's large enough to fit about 8 cups / 2 liters of liquid). The next day, to soaking mushrooms add cleaned and peeled celery root, carrots, parsnip, onion, peppercorns, allspice berries, and salt and simmer on low for 20 minutes. Strain the liquid and return it to the pot. Reserve the vegetables.

Strain beets that have been souring, reserving the water. Add ¼ cup of vinegar to them to prevent losing rich red color.

*Clean and peel fresh beets, slice thinly and add to mushroom / vegetable broth. Also add the beets from souring. Simmer for 5 minutes. Remove beets. Add sour beet water and heat up throughout, but **do not boil**.*

To finish off, add butter, marjoram, and crushed garlic. Taste. If it's too sour / vinegary, add a bit more sugar. Also add a bit more salt, if needed. Soup is ready!

23

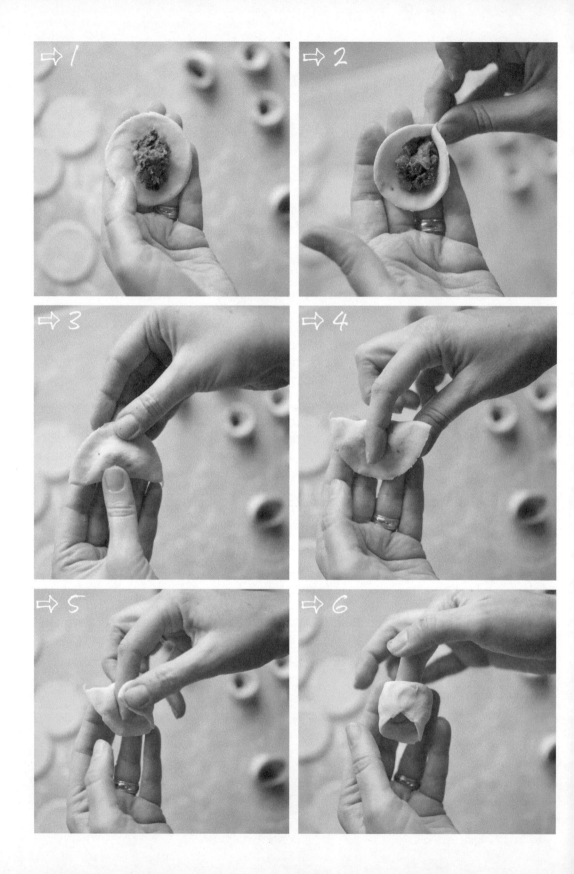

DUMPLING FILLING:

2 ½ c / 2 oz / 60 g of wild mushrooms*

8 oz / 250 g of baby portobello mushrooms or other fresh mushrooms

2 tsp of butter

1 large onion, minced

Pinch of salt and pepper

DOUGH:

3 c / 400 g of all-purpose flour

1 egg

1 ¼ c / 300 ml of warm water

1 tsp of salt

To make dumplings: if using wild mushrooms from preparing beet broth, just place cooked mushrooms in a food processor along with vegetables (carrots, parsnips, celery root) and blend until they're chopped, but not blended into paste.

If you're preparing dumplings without making beet broth, soak mushrooms overnight (or for at least 4 hours) in 2 ½ cups of water, then boil in the same water for about 20 minutes. Drain and set aside to cool. Once cooled off, place in a food processor and blend until finely chopped but not blended into paste. Wash baby portobellos and finely chop (or place in a food processor).

In a medium skillet, heat butter, add minced onion and portobellos, sprinkle with salt. Sauté until cooked and most of liquid has cooked off. Add chopped wild mushrooms and heat through until all liquid has cooked off. Taste. Add salt and pepper to taste. Set aside to cool.

Prepare dough by combining flour, egg, water, and salt, and kneading on a floured surface until smooth dough forms.

Fill a large pot with water, add about 1 teaspoon of salt and a splash of oil and start heating.

In batches, roll out dough to about ⅛ of an inch / 3 millimeter thickness.

With a small glass (about 2 inches / 5 centimeters in diameter), cut out circles. Fill each circle with about a ½ teaspoon of mushroom filling. Close each dumpling and press edges with a fork to seal.

Once sealed, gently stretch dumpling longways, wrap around one finger and pinch the two pointy ends together to form a round dumpling - see photos on the previous page.

After dropping into boiling water (in batches of about 20–30), stir gently off the bottom to prevent sticking. Turn heat down to low; water should only be slightly simmering (not rolling boil). When all dumplings float to the top, they are done. Remove from pot and place on a large surface to cool (without touching), or serve right away.

Christmas Mushroom Soup

—Wigilijna zupa grzybowa—

Creamy vegetarian broth with earthy tones of dried wild mushrooms served during Polish Christmas Eve dinner.

Yields: *5–6 servings* **Prep time:** *5 minutes + soaking* **Cook time:** *25 minutes*

1 oz / 30 g / 1 c of dried wild mushrooms*

1 ½ c / 350 ml of water for soaking

6 c / 1 ½ l of vegetable broth (or 6 c of water and the next 4 ingredients)

2 carrots

½ of celery root

¼ of an onion

1 parsnip or parsley root

6 whole peppercorns and allspice berries (each)

3 bay leaves

Salt (careful if using broth that may contain salt already)

2 tbsp of butter

2 tbsp of heavy cream

Soak wild mushrooms overnight (or at least 4 hours).

The next day, place mushrooms, with the water they were soaking in, in a medium pot. Add broth (or water and vegetables), spices and a pinch of salt. Boil covered on low for 30 minutes or until mushrooms are soft.

When wild mushrooms are cooked, strain everything out, reserve the liquid broth. Remove the vegetables (save to make a Polish vegetable salad "sałatka jarzynowa"), and, once the mushrooms cool, dice them and return to broth.

To cream add a bit of broth to temper it. Add cream to soup and heat through. Taste, add salt if needed and a sprinkle of fresh ground pepper.

Finish by adding butter for extra flavor.

Anna's note:

IMPORTANT: some wild mushrooms are not to be served to children. Do your research before serving to children.

27

Dill Soup with Drop Dumplings

—Zupa koperkowa i lane kluski—

Thick and creamy soup with small drop dumplings, garnished with garlic croutons and pumpkin seeds.

Yields: *8 servings* **Prep time:** *10 minutes* **Cook time:** *10 minutes*

— Soup —

2 qts / 2 l of vegetable or meat stock (or leftover chicken soup)

4–5 tbsp of fresh dill, chopped

¾ c / 175 ml of heavy cream

2 tbsp of all-purpose flour (or more for a thicker soup)

ADDITIONALLY:

A couple of pieces of bread for croutons

1 garlic clove

Pumpkin seeds for garnish

Bring stock to boil, add dill. Mix cream and flour well, no lumps. Add about ¼ cup of hot broth to cream / flour mixture to temper it, mix well. Repeat twice. Add mixture to soup. Bring to boil and keep on simmer.

— Dumplings —

1 egg

2 tbsp of all-purpose flour

Pinch of salt

Place egg in a medium bowl and whisk for about a minute until small bubbles form. Add a pinch of salt and flour, one tablespoon at a time. Whisk to combine.

Pour dumpling batter into soup in a thin stream. Whisk in soup to break up. Bring to boil.

Toast bread and rub with garlic clove. Cut into croutons and garnish the soup right before serving. Add pumpkin seeds for extra flavor.

Anna's note:

Double the dumplings recipe for thicker soup.

Anna's note:

If blood is not available in your area, try making this soup without. The main flavor of the soup comes from dried fruit, cherries and aromatic duck meat.

Duck Blood Soup

— Czarnina —

An "old school" delicacy, this aromatic soup mainly gets it's flavor from dried fruit and duck. The soup is also know as "czarna polewka" or "czernina".
This soup is often prepared during holidays or special occasions.

Yields: *6–8 servings* **Prep time:** *15 minutes* **Cook time:** *2 hours*

½ c of dried apples

10 prunes

¼ c of dried pears

4–5 dried wild mushrooms

1 duck - we'll use breast bones, neck and giblets only

3 carrots

1 parsnip or parsley root

½ a small leek

¼ of a small celery root and a few twigs of the leafy part

¼ of an onion, burnt over a gas stove or in a dry pan

6–7 c / 1 ½ liters of water

1 tbsp of salt

6 whole peppercorns and all-spice berries (each)

3–4 bay leaves

One 14.5 oz / 400 g can of tart cherries

1 tbsp of all-purpose flour

1 c / 230 ml of cold water

About ¾ c / 180–200 ml of duck blood*

1 tbsp of vinegar

Additional salt

½–1 tsp of sugar

Place dried fruit and mushrooms in 2 cups / 450 milliliters of water overnight (or for at least 1 hour).

Wash the duck, remove and set aside wings, breasts, and legs, leaving the breast bone, neck and gizzards to make a flavorful broth. If this is too difficult of a task, ask your butcher for help.

Place meat, bones, and vegetables in a medium pot and add water, salt, peppercorns, allspice berries, and bay leaves. Boil on low heat for 1 ½ hours. Remove meat and veggies from the pot and strain the broth.

Place broth back on heat. Add reconstituted fruit and mushrooms (with liquid) and tart cherries, simmer on low for about 10 minutes.

In the meantime, mix flour well with cold water (no clumps). Mix blood with vinegar and add to water / flour mixture. Pour into soup and bring to boil. Boil for about 3 minutes. Turn off. Taste; add a bit of salt and sugar if needed. Amount of sugar will depend on the level of sweetness in dried fruit and cherries. Soup should be slightly sweet and savory. Vinegar is not a super prevalent flavor in it. Add salt and sugar bit by bit to get to the desired flavor.

Serve hot, over thin pasta or homemade soup noodles.

Recipe for homemade soup noodles on page 69 !

Pearl Barley Soup

— Krupnik —

Krupnik is a relatively thick and mild savory soup, with the main flavor component coming from pearl barley. Potatoes, carrots, and parsley add a delicate sweetness, texture, and color.

Yields: *8 servings*   **Prep time:** *10 minutes*   **Cook time:** *20 minutes*

2 qts / 2 l of vegetable or meat stock (or leftover chicken soup)

½ c of pearl barley

1 large carrot

5 small potatoes

3 bay leaves

4–5 whole peppercorns and all-spice berries (each)

Parsley for garnish

Salt and pepper

1 tbsp of butter

Bring stock to boil.

Add barley, peeled and chopped carrot and cubed potatoes, bay leaves, peppercorns and allspice berries.

Add a teaspoon of salt (if the stock is unsalted). Boil for 15 minutes, until vegetables are soft and barley cooked.

Turn off, taste. Add more salt if needed.

Sprinkle with pepper and parsley.

Add butter and stir.

Serve.

Anna's note:

As soup sits it will thicken. Add more stock if too thick.

Pickle Soup

—Zupa ogórkowa—

*Sour savory broth balanced with potatoes and carrots,
garnished with fragrant fresh dill.*

Yields: *6 servings* **Prep time:** *10 minutes* **Cook time:** *40 minutes*

About 1 ½ lbs / 700 g of chicken (wings or other bone-in parts)

1 tsp salt

3 bay leaves

3 carrots

4–6 whole peppercorns and allspice berries (each)

3 medium potatoes

One 30 oz / 900 ml jar of pickles in brine*

3 tbsp of all-purpose flour

1 c / 230 ml of cold water

About 3 tbsp of fresh dill

Wash chicken parts and place in a medium pot with about 6–7 cups (1 ½ quarts) of water. Add salt, bay leaves, carrots, peppercorns and allspice berries. Boil on medium to medium-low heat for about 30–40 minutes (until chicken falls off the bone).

In the meantime, peel potatoes and cut into medium cubes. Keep in cold water.

Grate pickles on the medium side of a box grater, set aside. Cut up fresh dill.

When chicken is done, remove from stock and take off the bone. Also remove carrots and slice.

Add cubed potatoes to the stock and boil for about 10 minutes, or until soft.

When potatoes are soft, return meat and carrots to the pot. Add shredded pickles (I also like to add all of the brine to make my soup more sour).

In a small bowl or cup, combine cold water with flour, whisk well and add to the soup to thicken. Bring to boil and turn off.

Finally, add chopped fresh dill and serve.

Anna's note:

* *Pickles in brine are the fermented pickles in salt brine and can be found at almost any Polish grocery store in the US (or my recipe on page 204). If you can't find those, use your favorite dill pickles.*

Potato Soup

— Kartoflanka —

*Thick soup spiked with true Polish flavors
of smoked bacon and marjoram.*

Yields: *8 servings*   **Prep time:** *15 minutes*   **Cook time:** *30 minutes*

8 c / 1 ½ kg of raw or cooked potatoes, cubed

About 6 oz / 170 g of smoked pork (bacon, sausage, ham hock, or ham bone). Smoked turkey will also do.

1 ½ c of peeled and cubed carrots (3 large carrots)

1 parsnip or parsley root, peeled and cubed

¼ of a large celery root (or 1 celery stalk, sliced)

6 whole peppercorns and allspice berries (each)

2 bay leaves

8 c / 2 l of water

½ tbsp of salt

FOR ROUX:

3 tbsp of butter

¾ c of chopped onion

½ tbsp of marjoram

3 tbsp of all-purpose flour

If using raw potatoes, peel and cube them. If using leftover baked potatoes, cube them and set aside.

Place raw potatoes*, smoked meat, carrots, parsnip (or parsley root), celery, peppercorns, allspice berries, and bay leaves in a large pot. Add water and salt. Boil for about 20 minutes, or until veggies are soft.

*If using cooked potatoes, add them when the rest of the veggies are soft and heat through.

In a small sauté pan, make roux: melt butter, add chopped onion and sauté until lightly browned. Add marjoram and cook another minute. Add flour and whisk until well combined. Add a couple of cups of hot soup and whisk to combine. Transfer roux into pot and stir well until soup thickens. Serve.

Anna's note:

* You can use leftover smoked ribs, if not too sweet. You can also substitute smoked ribs with smoked pork belly/bacon. Find a good quality pork belly / bacon though, best if whole, not sliced.

Sauerkraut Soup with Pork Ribs

—Kwaśnica —

*Meaty and sour soup
that originated in the Polish mountain region.*

Yields: *8–10 servings*   **Prep time:** *10 minutes*   **Cook time:** *2.5–3 hours*

About 2 lbs / 900 g of raw pork baby back ribs

Salt and freshly ground pepper

2 tbsp of vegetable oil or lard

2 ½ qts / 2 ½ l of water

2 garlic cloves

4 bay leaves

10 whole peppercorns and all-spice berries (each)

About 1 lb / 500 g of smoked pork ribs or bacon*

About 1 lb / 500 g of raw potatoes

One 14 oz / 400 g can of sauerkraut

1 tbsp of dried marjoram

Wash raw pork ribs, pat dry and slice into individual ribs. Sprinkle with salt and pepper.

In a large stockpot, heat oil / lard. When ready, gently place each rib into hot oil, making sure there is enough room around it to brown (work in batches, if necessary). Brown ribs for a few minutes on each side. They do not have to cook through, just get a nice color.

Once browned, remove and add the next batch. Once all pieces are browned, return to pot, add water, crushed garlic cloves, bay leaves, peppercorns and allspice berries. Bring to boil, turn heat down and simmer on low for about 1 hour (until meat is tender).

In the meantime, cut smoked ribs / bacon into 1 inch / 3 centimeter chunks, also peel and dice potatoes, then keep in cold water until later.

When pork is tender, add smoked rib / bacon chunks and diced potatoes to the stock. Let simmer for another 30 minutes (until smoked ribs / bacon are soft).

Finally, add sauerkraut (with juices) and marjoram and simmer for another 15–20 minutes, or until kraut is cooked.

Serve with crusty bread, bacon, ribs and all!

Sorrel Soup

— Zupa szczawiowa —

Sorrel soup is a seasonal dish prepared primarly in the spring, when sorrel is in season in Poland. This sour vegetable makes a delicious, creamy and delicate soup.

Yields: *8 servings*   **Prep time:** *10 minutes*   **Cook time:** *40 minutes*

STOCK:

1 lb / 500g of bone-in chicken parts

8 c / 2 l of water

2 carrots

1 parsnip or parsley root

¼ of a small celery root or a couple of celery stalks

½ a small onion burnt in a dry pan or directly over gas stove

2 tsp of salt

3–4 bay leaves

6–8 whole peppercorns and allspice berries (each)

ADDITIONALLY:

1 lb / 500 g of fresh sorrel leaves

2 tbsp of butter

3 eggs

4 slices of bread (to make croutons)

1 garlic clove

Sprinkle of salt and pepper

Place stock ingredients in a stockpot and bring to boil. Simmer on low for 45 minutes. If using boxed stock, pour into a medium pot and heat up.

In the meantime, wash sorrel throughly, cut off and discard just the thickest stem ends. Mince sorrel finely. In a medium pan, heat butter, add sorrel and sauté for a few minutes until all liquid cooks off.

Boil eggs. Once boiled, peel and dice and set aside.

Toast bread and peel garlic. Rub the whole surface of each slice of toast with garlic clove. Dice and set aside.

Once stock is ready, strain it but return parsnip / parsley root and celery root back into the stock. Also, add ⅔ of sautéed sorrel into pot. With an immersion blender, blend the soup with vegetables.

Finally, dice carrots and add to soup. Add the rest of sorrel and heat through. Stir and taste. Sprinkle with freshly ground pepper and a bit more salt, if needed.

Right before serving, add diced egg and croutons.

Sour Rye Soup Starter

—Zakwas na żur —

*Fermented soup starter made from rye flour
provides a tangy soup base for "żurek".*

Yields: *4 cups / 1 liter*   **Prep time:** *10 minutes*   **Fermenting time:** *5-7 days*

½ c / 60 g of rye flour plus ½ c on day 3

2 c / 500 ml of boiled and cooled water (plus 2 c / 500 ml on day 3)

5 garlic cloves

3 bay leaves

6 whole peppercorns and all-spice berries (each)

1 tbsp of dried marjoram

1 qt / 1 l glass jar / container

Sanitize a glass container and cool enough to handle.

Mix cooled water with flour until combined.

Place all ingredients in your container and stir. Cover with kitchen towel or cheesecloth and let rest for 3 days at room temperature (60–75°F / 16–25°C).

On day 3, add remaining flour and water, stir well and let rest at room temperature for another 3–4 days.

Stir daily. When done, cover and refrigerate until ready to make "żurek" - recipe on page 45.

43

Sour Rye Soup

— Żurek —

Tangy and smoky soup, prepared with traditional Polish fresh sausage and served during Polish Easter.

Yields: *8–10 servings*   **Prep time:** *10 minutes*   **Cook time:** *20 minutes*

3 qts / 3 l of water

1 carrot

1 small parsley root

2 inch / 5 cm wedge of a celery root

6 oz / 200 g of smoked slab bacon (in one piece)

6 links of fresh Polish sausage (about 16 oz / 450 g) - recipe on pg. 127

1 tsp salt (more to taste)

4 c / 1 l sour rye starter - recipe on pg. 43*

3 tbsp of dried marjoram

2 garlic cloves, crushed

Sprinkle of ground black pepper

GARNISH:

6 hard-boiled eggs

5 tsp of prepared horseradish

Place all vegetables in a soup pot, add water, bacon, sausages, and salt. Bring to boil. Skim off all solids and simmer on low for 30 minutes.

With a slotted spoon, gently remove vegetables, bacon, and sausages. Cut sausages into 1–2 inch / 3–5 centimeter pieces.

To the stock add 4 cups / 1 liter of rye starter (strained), sausage pieces, marjoram (rub in between your fingers to bloom), and crushed garlic. Sprinkle with ground pepper and boil on low for 5 minutes, stirring often.

Taste and add a bit more salt, if needed.

Soup is ready but it will do best if it combines for a few hours or overnight.

When ready to serve, place two egg halves in each bowl, along with a few pieces of sausage.

Pour in hot soup and add a bit of horseradish to taste.

Serve with bread.

Anna's note:

"Instead of preparing your own starter, you can purchase a store-bought version at many Polish delis. Look for "Zakwas na Żur". You will need 2 (500 ml) bottles. Add more stock if too thick.

45

Tomato Soup

Zupa pomidorowa

Creamy soup with notes of sweet and tangy tomatoes. It is often prepared on Mondays using the leftover chicken broth "rosół" cooked on Sunday.

Yields: *6–8 servings*　**Prep time:** *5 minutes*　**Cook time:** *30 minutes*

About 2 qts / 2 l of chicken stock (or leftover chicken soup + chicken meat)

8 tomatoes (or one 14 oz / 410 ml can of stewed tomatoes)

One 5.5 oz / 156 ml can of tomato paste

2 carrots (if using boxed chicken stock)

1 tsp of sugar

¼ c / 60 ml of sweet cream

2 tbsp of butter

Pasta or rice for serving

Parsley for garnish

Place stock (or leftover chicken soup, without the meat) in a soup pot. Add stewed canned tomatoes and tomato paste and blend with an immersion blender.

Turn to boil. Add peeled carrots and cook uncovered until it thickens a bit, about 15 minutes on medium-low or low.

Taste. Add salt, if needed. If you have some leftover chicken meat, you may also add to soup to heat through.

Turn heat off, add sugar, cream, and butter.

Serve with pasta or rice, carrot slices and chicken meat, garnished with parsley.

Anna's note:

Best if soup sits overnight. To serve, reheat and serve very hot, with crusty bread.

Tripe Soup

— Placzki —

Aromatic beef tripe soup, prepared Polish style, with root vegetables and aromatic spices. This traditional soup is often referred to as "hangover soup".

Yields: *5–6 servings*   **Prep time:** *30 minutes*   **Cook time:** *3 hours*

1 lb / 500 g of beef tripe

2 carrots

1 parsnip or parsley root

¼ of a celery root

2 garlic cloves, crushed

½ a small onion

1 lb / 500 g of beef on the bone (ribs or tail)

½ tbsp of salt

3–4 bay leaves

6 whole peppercorns and allspice berries (each)

2 tbsp of butter

2 tbsp of flour

½ tsp of ground ginger

2 tsp of paprika

¼ tsp of ground nutmeg

1 tbsp of dried marjoram

More salt and freshly ground pepper or red pepper flakes

Wash tripe with cold water. Place in a pot and cover with water. Boil for 10 minutes. Drain and rinse well with cold water. Repeat this 3 times. Make sure the meat is clean and free of any impurities. If it still gives off **a strong** *smell, repeat one more time. In the meantime, peel carrots, parsnip / parsley root, celery root, and garlic. Peel onion and burn straight on a gas burner or a dry frying pan.*

After you've decided tripe is ready, place it and beef in the same pot. Add 6 cups / 1 ½ liters of water, salt, peeled carrots, parsnip / parsley root, celery root, garlic, and burnt onion. Also add bay leaves, peppercorns and allspice berries. Bring to boil, turn to low and simmer for 20 minutes, until vegetables are soft. Remove vegetables and continue boiling (covered) for another 2 hours.

In the meantime, grate vegetables on the largest side of the box grater, set aside.

After 2 hours of cooking tripe, taste a piece of tripe, if it's still not soft, continue boiling for another 30 minutes–1 hour. When done, remove beef bones and debone any meat that may have cooked on the bone and return meat to broth.

Lastly, in a small sautéing pan make roux by melting butter and combining with flour. Add about ½ cup of broth to roux and whisk to combine. Add to soup and bring to boil to thicken. Add grated vegetables, ginger, paprika, nutmeg, and marjoram. Boil for another 10 minutes. Taste.

Here, I added another tablespoon of salt, ½ teaspoon of freshly ground pepper, and a sprinkle of red pepper flakes. Soup should be salty and a bit spicy. Add more, if needed but do it gradually. It does need quite a bit of salt, though.

Young Beetroot Soup

— Botwinka —

Classic soup made from young beets and mixed vegetables prepared and served starting in early spring and enjoyed all through the summer when beets are in season.

Yields: *5-6 servings*   **Prep time:** *45 minutes*   **Cook time:** *30 minutes*

3-4 small young beets (roots, stems, and leaves)

About ½ lb / 500 g of pork ribs

Salt and pepper

1-2 tbsp of oil

2 qts / 2 l of water (or vegetable broth)

1 carrot

2 bay leaves

10 peppercorns, whole

2 tbsp of vinegar

2 tsp of sugar

A squeeze of lemon

ADDITIONALLY:

Sour cream

Parsley

Preheat oven to 350°F / 180°C. Cut leaves off the beets at the stem. Wash roots and bake roots only, covered, for about 30 minutes - small beets; 45 minutes - medium beets and close to 60 minutes - large beets.

Wash and dry pork ribs. Sprinkle with salt and pepper and sear in a bit of grease on medium heat until golden brown.

Heat water (or broth) and add seared ribs, carrots and spices. Boil on low heat for about 30 minutes.

Cut washed beet stems and leaves into about 0.5 inch / 2 centimeter pieces. Add to soup and boil for another 5-7 minutes, until stems are soft.

Cool cooked beets, peel them and cut into similar pieces. Add to soup along with vinegar, sugar, and lemon juice and heat through.

Don't boil*. Taste and add salt, if needed.

Serve hot, with a dollop of sour cream and a sprinkle of parsley.

Anna's note:

*Cooking beets rids them of the bright red color. Once beets are in, try not to boil this soup too much.

Pierogi
Dumplings
Pancakes

Pierogi, kluski, placki

Perfect Pierogi Dough

Yields: *55–60 dumplings*   **Prep time:** *5 minutes*

— Traditional Pierogi Dough —

3 c / 375 g of all-purpose flour
1 tsp of salt
1 egg
1 ¼ c / 300 ml of warm water

Start by placing egg and salt in a bowl and whisking lightly.

Add flour and water. Mix until ingredients combine and form a dough ball. Knead only until well combined (about 2–3 minutes).

— Vegan Pierogi Dough —

3 c / 375 g of all-purpose flour
1 tsp of salt
2 tbsp of oil
1 ¼ c / 300 ml of warm water

To make the dough, place flour and salt in a bowl first, whisk lightly.

Add oil and water. Mix until ingredients combine and form a dough ball. Knead only until well combined (about 2–3 minutes).

— Freezing & Reheating Pierogi —

TO FREEZE: *spread boiled and cooled pierogi on a baking sheet (not touching), and place in the freezer. After they are frozen, transfer to a zip-top bag.*

TO REHEAT: *place in a shallow pan with a bit of butter and a small splash of water. Heat covered on low until dumplings are hot (about 5 minutes), then uncover and brown on each side.*

Homemade Farmer's Cheese

— Twaróg —

Traditional soft cheese, tangy in flavor, is used in cooking (pierogi filling, cheesecake) or enjoyed as breakfast mixed with dill or chives.

Yields: *1 lb / 500 g*   **Prep time:** *72 hours*   **Cook time:** *60 minutes*

1 gal / 4 l of full fat milk
1 c / 250 ml of buttermilk*
ADDITIONALLY:
Cheesecloth
Strainer

Disinfect a glass or ceramic container big enough to fit 1 gallon / 4 liters of milk + 1 cup / 250 ml of buttermilk using hot water. Pour milk and buttermilk into it and set on the counter covered with a clean kitchen towel for 72 hours (or more).

When milk becomes solid (and is no longer "slimy") to where you can slice it and it will stay separated, it is ready. Consistency should resemble sour cream or Greek yogurt.

Pour into a large soup pot, cover and heat on the lowest heat setting until whey separates from curds and the curds start hardening. Don't stir. Cook for about 1 hour. Curds should be a bit hard, kind of like cottage cheese. If still mushy, keep heating slowly.

When "cooked", place cheesecloth over a strainer and pour liquid through. Let sit for about 10 minutes to drain. To get rid of extra liquid, twist cheesecloth to squeeze it out. Leave some moisture though; you don't want it too dry.

When satisfied with the moisture level, transfer into a container and refrigerate.

Anna's note:

* If using unpasteurized milk, skip adding buttermilk.

Anna's note:
To serve, top with sour cream and a sprinkle of sugar.

Berry Pierogi

– Pierogi z jagodami –

Fruit-filled pierogi usually made during the summer using a favorite seasonal berry.

Yields: *55–60 dumplings* **Prep time:** *25 minutes* **Cook time:** *45 minutes*

2 lbs / 1 kg of fresh (or frozen) blueberries or strawberries

DOUGH:

3 c / 375 g of all-purpose flour

1 tsp of salt

1 egg

1 ¼ c / 300 ml of warm water

ADDITIONALLY:

Sour cream

Sugar

To make the dough, place egg and salt in a bowl first, whisk lightly. Add flour and water. Mix until ingredients combine and form a dough ball. Knead only until well combined (about 2–3 minutes). Take out a portion of it (about a third) onto a floured surface and roll out to about ⅛ inch / 2 millimeter thickness.

Cut out about 3 inch / 6–7 centimeter circles with the brim of a glass. Place 5–8 blueberries or 2–3 halves of strawberry on each circle and sprinkle with a pinch of sugar. Fold in half and seal the edges. Wet the edges lightly to help with the seal. Use a fork to go around the outside of the edge, if you'd like, or make a decorative edge.

Lay out on a floured surface until ready to boil.

Do the same with the rest of the dough.

Simmer on low in a large pot of water with a table-spoon of oil and a tablespoon of salt until they all float to the top. Don't place too many in the pot at a time.

Remove from pot and spread on a large surface to cool (not touching), or serve right away topped with sour cream and a sprinkle of sugar.

Braised Cabbage & Dumplings

—łazanki z kapustą —

Soft, large and flat dumplings mixed with cabbage and bacon.

Yields: *8–10 servings*　**Prep time:** *10 minutes*　**Cook time:** *45 minutes*

6 oz / 175 g of good quality smoked bacon

1 large onion

½ head of medium cabbage

2 c / 500 ml of water

1 tbsp of salt

DUMPLINGS:

3 c / 375 g of all-purpose flour

1 egg

Pinch of salt

1 ¼ c / 300 ml of warm water

ADDITIONALLY:

2 + 4 tbsp of butter

3 tbsp of all-purpose flour

3–4 tbsp of fresh dill

Dice bacon and onion. Heat medium pan, add bacon and sauté until fat has melted. Add onion and sauté until both golden brown.

In the meantime, chop cabbage into relatively small pieces. I cut it into thin slices first, then into smaller bits. Heat water in a large pot, add cabbage and salt and boil for 5–7 minutes, until cabbage is soft, but still a bit crunchy.

When bacon and onions are ready, add to pot with cabbage. Mix until combined, turn heat off.

Set a large pot of water on for boiling dumplings now. We want the water to be ready right when the dumplings are made.

To make dumplings, place flour, egg, and salt in a mixing bowl. Start adding water and mix until a ball forms; if it gets too wet, add a bit more flour.

When all ingredients combine, transfer dough onto floured surface and knead until smooth (about 3 minutes). Divide into three parts. Roll out with a rolling pin and cut into strips and then diagonally (see photos on next page).

Sprinkle dumplings with flour and, with the help of your knife, lift them off of your surface, so they do not stick together.

*When water is boiling, slide them off your cutting board into the pot and **immediately** stir gently. We don't want them clumping together.*

Turn heat down and let simmer until dumplings float to the top. Drain and set aside.

Dump boiling water out, add a couple of tablespoons of butter to the same pot and add dumplings (this is a secret trick from my grandma; makes the dumplings even better)! Sauté for a few minutes, stir gently and often, until they get a little color.

Heat a small pan, add butter. Once melted, add flour. Mix until it becomes a smooth and bubbly roux, about 2 minutes.

Return cabbage to heat. Add roux to cabbage and mix well. Also add dumplings and mix. You might have to add a bit of water at this point. Cabbage should be moist but not saucy. You can easily add about a cup of water.

Taste, add a bit more salt and pepper, if needed. Sprinkle with chopped dill.

Serve hot.

Drop Dumplings

– Kluski kładzione –

*Doughy dumplings
best served with sauce.*

Yields: *5–6 servings* **Prep time:** *10 minutes* **Cook time:** *20 minutes*

3 c / 375 g of all-purpose flour
2 whole eggs
1 tsp of salt
1 ¼ c / 300 ml of warm water
Splash of oil

In a small bowl, beat eggs to mix yolks with whites. Place flour in a large mixing bowl, add eggs and salt. Slowly start adding water and beat on low until blended well.

Fill a large pot with water and bring to boil. Add a couple of tablespoons of salt and a splash of oil to the water.

With a metal soup spoon, scoop dumplings the size of a walnut and drop into the boiling water by submerging the spoon in the water. Do it in three batches, not to overcrowd the pot. Once dumplings are dropped, with a wooden spoon, gently stir the water to make sure dumplings aren't sticking together.

Turn water to low simmer and boil for 3–4 minutes from the moment they float to the top.

Remove with a slotted spoon and place in a colander. Sprinkle with a tiny bit of oil to prevent from sticking if not serving right away.

Anna's note:

To reheat, sauté in butter or drop into simmering water for 1 minute.

Farmer's Cheese Pierogi

– Pierogi z serem –

*Pierogi filled with sweet farmer's cheese
served with sugared sour cream.*

Yields: *55-60 dumplings*   **Prep time:** *25 minutes*   **Cook time:** *45 minutes*

DOUGH:

3 c / 375 g of all-purpose flour

1 whole egg

1 tsp of salt

1 ¼ c / 300 ml of warm water

FILLING:

2 lbs / 1 kg of farmer's cheese

2 egg yolks

½ tsp of salt

½ tbsp of sugar

¼ tsp cinnamon

GARNISH:

Sour cream and sugar

ADDITIONALLY:

Oil

Salt

To make dough, place flour, egg, and salt in a mixing bowl. If you're using a stand mixer, using the hook attachment, make dough by adding water bit by bit. If working by hand, also slowly add water until dough clumps. Then, transfer onto floured surface and work until smooth. Cover in plastic and set aside.

To make the filling, place farmer's cheese in the bowl of a food processor. Add egg yolks, salt, sugar, and cinnamon. Process well until lumps are gone.

Place a portion of the dough on a floured surface and roll it out with a rolling pin to about ⅛ inch / 2 millimeters in thickness. With a glass or a pierogi cutter, cut out circles, place filling on each circle and close to form pierogi.

Fill a large pot with water and set to boil. When water starts boiling, turn down to low, add a splash of oil and a pinch of salt. Drop dumplings into the water in batches (7–10 at a time). Stir gently and let float. When they float up to the top, let sit for about 2–3 minutes. Don't let the water roll; it may break your dumplings, and we don't want that.

Remove from pot and spread on a large surface to cool (not touching), or serve right away.

Pierogi freezing instructions on page 55 !

Anna's note:

To serve, top with sour cream and a sprinkle of sugar.

67

Homemade Soup Noodles

— Makaron domowy —

Homemade pasta to be served with a favorite soup.
To me they taste best with chicken soup or "czarnina" (duck blood soup).

Yields: *15–20 servings* **Prep time:** *15 minutes* **Cook time:** *45 minutes*

3 c / 375 g of all-purpose flour
3 whole eggs
1 tsp of salt
6–8 tbsp of warm water
More flour for rolling

Combine all ingredients until a dough forms, roll out thin and cut into strips about 6 inches / 15 centimeters wide.

Let strips dry a bit, for about 10 minutes.

Flour each strip heavily and roll into a tube. Flatten tube and slice into desired thickness.

*Boil right away in salted water for 3–5 minutes **or** spread in a single layer on a well-floured surface and let dry (uncooked) until completely dry, for at least 24 hours.*

Move pasta around a few times to prevent sticking.

Store in a non-airtight container.

When ready to consume, boil in salted water as you would store-bought pasta.

Anna's note:

Uncooked / dried pasta will store for weeks. Keep in a breathable container.

Anna's note:

Sometimes the type of farmer's cheese I buy is very dry and hard to break up. By dry, I mean it's like a brick of cheese, one that you can easily cut and it will keep its shape. If this is the case for you, add a few tablespoons of cream.

"Lazy" Pierogi

— Pierogi leniwe —

*Farmer's cheese dumplings
served with buttered bread crumbs and sugar.*

Yields: *15–20 dumplings*   **Prep time:** *15 minutes*   **Cook time:** *45 minutes*

1 lb / 500 g of farmer's cheese
3 eggs
Pinch of salt
1–1 ½ c / 125–190 g of all-purpose flour

ADDITIONALLY:
Salt
Oil
3–4 tbsp of butter
3–4 tbsp of bread crumbs
Sugar

Crumble farmer's cheese into a bowl, add eggs and salt. Use a hand mixer to break up the cheese and mix with eggs until fairly broken up (there will be visible lumps of cheese).

Add about 1 cup / 135 grams of flour and fold in with your hands. When it combines a bit, transfer onto a well floured board or other clean surface. Keep folding until dough forms, don't knead. If still too loose, add a bit more flour. Dough should be soft, but keep form.

Fill a large pot with water about half way, add about a ½ teaspoon of salt and a splash of oil and set to boil.

*Place bread crumbs in a small pan (dry) and toast until golden brown. **Watch this part!** They will burn quickly if not stirred. Add butter and stir until combined. Turn off and set aside.*

Divide dough into 3 parts and form a log by rolling against the board back and forth with your hands pressing lightly. When desired thickness is achieved (2 inches / 4 centimeters), lightly flatten the log and cut into pieces at an angle.

When the water starts boiling, turn the heat down and add about half of your batch. Lightly stir to prevent from sticking to the bottom. When dumplings start to float, boil on very low for about 2 minutes. Serve immediately, garnished with buttery bread crumbs and a sprinkle of sugar.

Meat Croquettes

—Krokiety z mięsem —

Savory Polish pancakes "naleśniki" with meat filling, breaded and fried.
They are normally served with aromatic beetroot broth.

Yields: *20–22 croquettes* **Prep time:** *10 minutes* **Cook time:** *20 minutes*

PANCAKES:

3 eggs

Pinch of salt

¾ c / 175 ml of buttermilk*

¾ c / 175 ml of milk

1 ⅓ c / 300 ml of water

2 tbsp of melted butter or oil

2 c /250 g of all-purpose flour

FILLING:

Meat of whole boiled chicken**

1 c of diced onion

3 tbsp of butter or oil

2 garlic cloves, minced

1 tbsp of dried marjoram

Salt & pepper to taste

ADDITIONALLY:

5 eggs

1 c of bread crumbs

Oil and butter for frying

Serve hot with a cup of beetroot broth – recipe on page 23.

To prepare "naleśniki", lightly beat eggs with salt, add the rest of ingredients and blend until it makes a smooth liquid batter.

Heat a non-stick pan with a tiny bit of butter over medium heat.

Pour about ⅓ cup of batter onto the pan and move pan around to spread batter to form an extra thin pancake.

When the top of the batter dries and the edges start curling up, flip. If the pancake falls apart while flipping add a couple of tablespoons of flour and whisk well. Cook for another minute or two, until golden brown. Remove from pan, set aside.

Take chicken off the bone and mince in a food processor or a meat grinder. Also grind all veggies from the soup (carrots, parsnip / parsley root, leek). Sauté onion in butter, and along with garlic, add to the filling. Also add salt, pepper, and marjoram to taste.

Fill each "naleśnik" by placing a scoop of filling towards the bottom of the circle. Fold pancake over the filling from the bottom up, then from each side into the middle (like a burrito). Roll forward to form a log. Set aside.

Prepare two separate shallow bowls, one for egg wash and one for bread crumbs. When all croquettes are ready, heat up a pan, add about a tablespoon each of butter and oil. Roll each croquette in egg wash and then in bread crumbs. Place in hot pan and sauté on low heat until golden brown. You can place the first batch in a warm oven to keep warm until you're done with the rest of croquettes.

Meat-filled Potato Dumplings

– Pyzy z mięsem –

Soft potato dumplings filled with a mixture of pork & beef.

Yields: *15 dumplings*   **Prep time:** *30 minutes*   **Cook time:** *30 minutes*

– Filling –

FILLING:

½ lb / 250 g of pork shoulder

½ lb / 250 g of stew beef

½ tsp of salt

½ tsp of pepper

½ tsp of onion powder

2 garlic cloves, crushed

Oil for sautéing

½ of a large onion, chopped

1 tbsp of butter / oil

½ c / 120 ml of chicken, beef or vegetable broth

¼ tsp of salt

¼ tsp of pepper

2 more garlic cloves, minced

½ tbsp of marjoram

To make the filling: sprinkle salt, pepper, and onion powder over cubed pork and beef, add crushed garlic. Sauté in a couple tablespoons of oil until cooked and edges of the meat are golden brown. Set aside to cool.

Sauté the onion until golden brown. Set aside to cool.

When meat cools off, mince in a food processor or meat grinder. When smooth, add broth, sautéed onion, salt, pepper, garlic and marjoram. Mix well to combine. Taste, and add more salt if needed.

Continued on the next page.

– Dumplings –

DOUGH:

2 lbs / 1 kg of boiled potatoes

1 lb / 500 g of raw potatoes

¼ of an onion

1 egg

A pinch of salt

¾ c /140 g of potato flour

¾ c / 90 g of all-purpose flour

Boil peeled potatoes (or use leftover potatoes). Set aside to cool. When cooled off, mash with a hand masher (or use a potato press) until smooth.

Place raw potatoes, onion and ¼ cup of water in a blender and blend until smooth. Place a cheesecloth over a strainer and pour raw potato mixture into it. Let drain for a few minutes. Twist the cloth and squeeze some of the water out, but not all.

Add raw potato mixture to boiled mashed potatoes, add egg, a pinch of salt, and both flours. Mix to form dough. It should be pretty sticky but not fall apart.

Using a ¼ cup measuring cup or an ice-cream scoop, scoop potato mixture onto your hand and form a circle. Fill the circle with as much meat as you can fit, and fold the sides of the circle up to close the dumpling (see photos). When closed, roll in your palms to even out the balls.

Fill a large pot with water, add salt and a splash of oil and bring to boil. Drop dumplings into boiling water in batches. Stir gently and boil on low for about 5 minutes from the time the water starts bubbling.

Take out and serve immediately, garnished with sautéed onion. If serving later, spread them on an oiled surface so they don't stick. To reheat, drop in simmering water for 2–3 minutes.

Anna's note:

This is a good weekend recipe as they take a little bit of time to prepare.

Meat-filled Soup Dumplings

— Kołduny —

Meat-filled dumplings usually served with chicken or duck broth.

Yields: *90 small dumplings* **Prep time:** *30 minutes* **Cook time:** *10 minutes*

FILLING:

2 ½ lbs / 1200 g of boneless raw ham (or other raw lean meat of choice)

2 tsp salt

2 garlic cloves, minced

½ tsp freshly ground pepper

1 tsp dried marjoram

½ tsp paprika

DOUGH:

3 c / 375 g of all-purpose flour

1 egg

1 ¼ c / 300 ml of warm water

1 tsp of salt

GARNISH:

Sour cream

Chives or parsley

Cut meat into smaller cubes and put through a grinder with the smallest grinding plate. Add salt, garlic, and all spices and mix well to incorporate. Set aside.

Prepare dough by combining flour, egg, water, and salt and kneading on a floured surface until smooth dough forms (about 2–3 minutes).

Fill a large pot with water, add about 1 teaspoon of salt and a splash of oil and start heating.

In batches, roll out dough to about ⅛ of an inch / 2 millimeter thickness.

With a small glass (about 2 inches / 5 centimeters in diameter), cut out circles. Fill each circle with about a teaspoon of raw meat filling. Close each dumpling and press edges with a fork or create a decorative seal.

Once sealed, place on a floured surface.

Drop into boiling water (in batches of 20) and stir gently off the bottom to prevent sticking. Turn heat down to low; water should only be slightly simmering (not rolling boil).

When all dumplings float to the top, let simmer on low for another 3 minutes. Remove from pot and spread on a large surface to cool (not touching), or serve right away.

Anna's note:

To reheat, place in a pan with a bit of butter and slowly brown on both sides.

Meat-filled Pierogi

— Pierogi z mięsem —

Dumplings with pork and beef filling flavored with garlic and marjoram, garnished with sautéed onions.

Yields: *100 dumplings* **Prep time:** *1.5 hours* **Cook time:** *5 minutes*

FILLING:

4 lbs / 2 kg of beef chuck and pork roast

Salt and pepper

Garlic powder

2 c / 500 ml of broth from cooking meat (or beef broth)

1 large onion

2 tbsp + 4 tbsp of butter

1 tsp of salt

1 ¼ tsp of freshly ground pepper

1 tbsp of marjoram

3 garlic cloves

DOUGH:

6 c / 750 g of all-purpose flour

2 eggs

2 tsp of salt

2 ½ c / 600 ml of warm water

Pierogi freezing instructions on page 55!

Wash and dry meat. Sprinkle lightly with salt, pepper, and garlic powder. Cook in 350°F / 180°C degree oven until cooked through. Take out and set aside to cool, remembering to reserve broth from cooking.

In the meantime, chop the onion and sauté in 2 tablespoons of butter.

Once meat cools, cube and put through a meat grinder with the smallest grinding plate.

To ground meat, add broth from roasting (about 2 cups; if not enough broth was produced, add water or boxed broth), sautéed onion, melted butter (4 tablespoons), salt, pepper, marjoram, and minced garlic.

Mix well. Taste. Add salt, if needed. Set aside.

To make dough, add whisked eggs and salt to flour. Start adding water and combining to form dough. Knead until smooth (about 3 minutes).

Put a large pot full of salted water on to boil. Add a splash of oil, to prevent sticking.

In batches, roll out dough to about ⅛ of an inch / 2 millimeter thickness. With a glass, cut out circles. Fill each circle with about a 1 ½ teaspoons of filling (or more if you'd like), close each dumpling and press edges with a fork to seal.

Drop into boiling water, turn heat down to low and, with a spoon, lightly stir off the bottom, to prevent sticking. Water should only be slightly simmering (not rolling boil). When all pierogi float to the top, they are done. Remove from pot and spread on a large surface to cool (not touching), or serve topped with sautéed onion.

Pancakes

—Naleśniki —

*Thin pancakes
with sweet and tangy farmer's cheese filling.*

Yields: *15–17 pancakes*   **Prep time:** *10 minutes*   **Cook time:** *40 minutes*

BATTER:

2 eggs

Pinch of salt

½ c / 120 ml of buttermilk*

½ c / 120 ml of milk

1 c / 250 ml of water

1 tbsp of melted butter

2 tsp of sugar

1 ½ c / 190 g of all-purpose flour

1 tsp of oil / butter for frying

FILLING:

8 oz / 220 g of farmer's cheese
(or cream cheese, softened)

½–¾ c of plain yogurt or sour
cream (skip if using cream
cheese)

1 tbsp of sugar (or more if you
like it sweeter)

½ tsp of cinnamon

Beat eggs with salt, add the remaining ingredients (except oil) and blend until it makes a smooth liquid batter.

Heat a non-stick medium pan with a tiny bit of butter / oil (medium heat).

Pour about ½ cup of batter onto the pan and move pan around to distribute into a thin layer.

When the top of the batter dries and the edges start curling up, flip.

Cook for another minute or two, until golden brown. Remove from pan, set aside.

Mix together ingredients for the filling to make a thick paste.

Spread a portion of the cheese mixture onto each "naleśnik", fold in half and in half again.

They are ready to be served, but I like to sauté mine in a tiny bit of butter. They get crispy on the outside and the filling warms up a bit.

Anna's note:

* If you don't have buttermilk, just use regular milk, but it's so worth using buttermilk.

83

Poppyseed Noodles

—Kluski z makiem —

Sweet poppyseeds with raisins and nuts, served with noodles is a dish usually prepared for Polish Christmas Eve dinner.

Yields: *6–10 servings* **Prep time:** *1 hour* **Cook time:** *10 minutes*

⅔ c / 100 g / 4 oz of raisins

7 oz / 200 g of raw poppyseeds

1 c / 250 ml of water

3 tbsp of honey

Pinch of salt

2 tbsp of butter

1 c / 100 g / 4 oz of walnuts

DUMPLINGS:

1 ½ c / 190 g of all-purpose flour

1 egg

½–⅔ c / 100–150 ml of warm water

Place raisins in a container and cover with warm water. Set aside to soak.

Place poppyseeds in a medium saucepan and add enough warm water to cover, set aside to soak for about 10 minutes, then boil for 20–25 minutes. Add a bit more water if they get dry, enough to cover. After 25 minutes, drain well.

Fill a medium-large pot with water, add a teaspoon of salt and a splash of oil and bring to boil.

In the meantime, make dumplings by combining all ingredients in the mixing bowl of a stand mixer and mix with a hook attachment. If you are working by hand, mix all ingredients in a mixing bowl.

When combined, transfer onto a clean, floured surface (preferably a large cutting board) and knead until smooth. Roll out with a rolling pin and cut into strips (a pizza cutter works great!) and then diagonally (see photos on the next page).

Sprinkle dumplings with flour and, with the help of your knife, lift them off of your surface, so they do not stick together. When water is boiling, slide them off your cutting board into the pot and **immediately** stir gently; we don't want them clumping together. Turn heat down and let simmer until dumplings float to the top. Drain and set aside to cool.

*Now, we will work on the poppyseeds. Once they cool slightly you will have to put them through a meat grinder with the fine grinding plate - **twice!***

Once you've done that, place ground poppyseeds in a medium pot, add: water (1 cup / 250 ml), honey, and a pinch of salt, and also water from soaking raisins. Simmer on low until water evaporates. Lastly, add butter and stir to melt and incorporate.

Transfer poppyseed mixture to a large bowl, add raisins, walnuts and dumplings. Mix to combine. Dish can be served cold or warm.

Potato & Cheese Pierogi

– Pierogi ruskie –

*Classic pierogi
with a potato and farmer's cheese filling.*

Yields: *55-60 dumplings* **Prep time:** *1 hour* **Cook time:** *5 minutes*

FILLING:

2 lbs / 1 kg of raw potatoes

16 oz / 500 g of farmer's cheese (or 16 oz / 500 g cottage cheese - drained + 3–4 tbsp of plain greek yogurt)

1 large onion

2 tbsp of butter

1 tsp of salt

1 tsp of freshly ground pepper

DOUGH:

3 c / 375 g of all-purpose flour

1 tsp of salt

1 egg

1 ¼ c / 300 ml of warm water

GARNISH:

½ an onion

A couple of strips of bacon chopped and sautéed into bacon bits (optional)

Pierogi freezing instructions on page 55 !

To make the filling, peel and boil potatoes in salted water until soft. Drain and set aside to cool.

Mince the onion and sauté in butter until golden brown.

If using farmer's cheese, crumble with a fork and set aside. If using cottage cheese, place in a strainer to strain some of the liquid.

When potatoes cool, mash with a hand masher, add sautéed onion, cheese (if using American cottage cheese, add plain greek yogurt), salt and pepper. Mix until combined. Taste and add salt, if needed.

Next, combine all ingredients to make the dough. Roll out in batches into about ⅛ inch / 2 millimeters in thickness. With a glass rim, cut out circles. Place a dollop of filling in each circle and seal tightly. Wet the inside of the edge for a better seal, and press edges with a fork once sealed or create a decorative edge.

Fill a large pot with water, add a tablespoon each of salt and oil. Once water starts boiling, turn down to **low**. Place a few dumplings (about 10, not to overcrowd) into boiling water, and **lightly** stir, to prevent sticking. Let boil for about 3 minutes, until they all float up to the top. Take out and spread on a clean surface, not touching.

You can serve immediately garnished with sautéed onion and bacon bits or sauté in butter on both sides until golden brown, garnished also with onion and bacon bits. Bacon bits are optional, but very desirable.

89

Silesian Potato Dumplings

—Kluski śląskie—

*Doughy and bouncy potato dumplings best served with a meat sauce.
They originated in Poland's Silesia region. In Poland they are humorously called
Silesian dumplings with a hole - "kluski śląskie z dziurką".*

Yields: *about 30 dumplings* **Prep time:** *20 minutes* **Cook time:** *10 minutes*

2 lbs / 1 kg of potatoes

3 strips of thick-cut smoked bacon

1 onion

½ c / 90 g of potato flour (or corn starch)

½ c / 60 g of all-purpose flour

½ tsp of salt

Wash, peel and boil potatoes in salted water.

Dice bacon and onion and sauté until golden brown on the edges.

Fill a large pot with water, add a teaspoon of salt and a splash of oil. Set to boil.

When potatoes are soft, drain and, while still hot, transfer to a bowl. With an electric hand mixer, mix potatoes for about 1 minute until all broken apart. Add flours and salt and blend for another 20 seconds.

Transfer dough to a well-floured surface and fold until a dough ball forms; don't knead, just fold. Dough will be quite wet; add a bit more flour to prevent from sticking.

Cut a piece off, roll out to form a 2 inch / 5 centimeter in diameter log, cut log into pieces about 1 inch long. Roll each piece in your hands to form a ball. Flatten the ball slightly. With the end of a knife or a spatula, make an indentation in the dumpling.

Once water is boiling, add dumplings (in 2 batches), and simmer on low for about 1 minute from the time they float to the top. Don't overdo this part. They will start falling apart if boiled too long.

Remove from pot and spread on a large surface to cool (not touching), or serve right away.

Anna's note:

Serve with bacon bits and onion or a meaty sauce.

Potato Dumplings

—Kopytka—

Doughy potato dumplings
best served with creamy sauce.

Yields: *4–5 servings* **Prep time:** *10 minutes* **Cook time:** *15 minutes*

1 lb / 500 g of cooked and cooled potatoes (leftovers are great!)

1 egg

1 c / 125 g of all-purpose flour

1 tsp of salt

Fill a large pot with water, salt it with a teaspoon of salt, and add a tablespoon of oil.

Mash potatoes with a potato masher in a pot. Measure out flour onto a clean surface, add potatoes, whisked egg, and salt and fold together gently. Do not knead. Dough will be slightly wet. Add a tablespoon of flour to keep from sticking to your hands, if needed.

Fold just until combined, not more than 1–2 minutes.

Cut away ¼ of the dough and roll to form a long log. Flatten the log and cut it into 1–1 ½ inch / 3–4 centimeter pieces at a 45-degree angle.

Place raw dumplings in boiling water in batches (2 batches, if using a 6 quart pot), stir gently to prevent dumplings from sticking to the bottom and to each other.

Simmer on low for about 1 minute from the time they start floating to the top (about 3 minutes total). Remove from pot and spread on a large surface to cool (not touching), or serve right away.

Anna's note:

To reheat, place in a pan with butter. Brown on all sides. These soft dumplings are great with a creamy meat sauce or a mushroom sauce.

93

Potato Dumplings with Plums

– Knedle ze śliwkami –

Sweet, potato dumplings filled with ripe plums.

Yields: *15 dumplings*   **Prep time:** *1 hour*   **Cook time:** *5 minutes*

– Dumplings –

6–7 medium potatoes or 2 c of leftover mashed potatoes

1 c / 125 g of all-purpose flour + a couple of handfuls for folding

2 eggs

Pinch of salt

About ½ lb / 250 g of ripe plums

If starting with raw potatoes, peel, wash and boil them, then mash and set aside to cool.

In the meantime, wash plums and cut into pieces (about 1 inch / 3 centimeters). Fill a large pot with water, add a pinch of salt and a splash of oil and bring to boil. Turn to low.

Once potatoes have cooled off, place them in a large bowl or a clean surface, add flour, eggs, and salt and fold to form dough. It will get pretty sticky; add a handful or two of flour and fold some more. With your hands, roll into a log about 2 inches / 5 centimeters in diameter, and cut into squares - see photos. Flatten each square and, with your fingers, form a circle. Place a couple of pieces of cut up plum onto the circle and fold the sides up to close around the fruit. Roll between your palms gently to seal and form an even round ball. Set aside and continue until all dough is filled.

Continued on the next page.

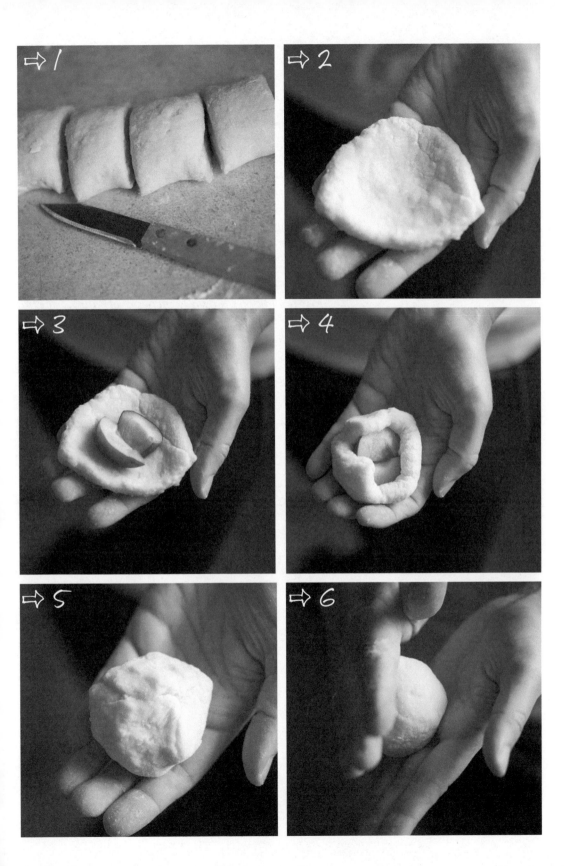

3–4 tbsp of bread crumbs

3–4 tbsp of butter

Drop into boiling water (in batches of about 5–6 dumplings) and gently stir water around them to prevent from sticking to the bottom and each other. Boil on medium-low for 3 minutes from the time they float to the top. Water should not be at a full roll. After 3 minutes, remove one and test to make sure the inside of the dumpling is cooked. If so, remove with a strainer and set on a cookie sheet or a large plate.

To prepare the topping, heat a small frying pan on medium-high. To the dry pan, add bread crumbs and toast until lightly brown (watch closely; they will burn fast). Turn heat to low or off and add butter. Mix until butter and bread crumbs combine.

Serve "knedle" warm, covered with bread crumb / butter mixture and a sprinkle of sugar.

Potato Pancakes

—Placki ziemniaczane—

*Thin, pan fried potato pancakes traditionally served with sour cream and sugar
or any kind of meat or mushroom sauce.*

Yields: *16–20 pancakes* **Prep time:** *10 minutes* **Cook time:** *20 minutes*

2 lbs / 1 kg of raw potatoes

1 onion

2 eggs

½ c / 60 g of all-purpose flour

2 tsp of salt

½ c / 120 ml of water (if needed)

Grease (oil or lard) for frying

ADDITIONALLY:

Sour cream and sugar for topping

Peel and rough dice the potatoes and onion (be prompt; you don't want the potatoes turning brown) and place in your blender (I needed to put some water with the veggies to get it going, but it's not necessary if you have a high-speed super blender). I did this in two batches. Make sure to leave some onion for both batches: it prevents the raw potatoes from turning brown. Blend on high for a couple of minutes to create a smooth paste.

Put a colander lined with cheesecloth over a bowl. Transfer your mixture into the colander and let it sit for a few minutes to drain some of the liquid. You may also bring the edges of the cheesecloth together to squeeze it out. Reserve the liquid.

Transfer potato / onion mixture into a bowl, add lightly beaten eggs, flour, and salt.

On the bottom of the liquid that collected in the bowl, you will see a thin layer of potato starch. Slowly pour the liquid out, but leave the starch behind and add it to your potato / onion mixture. Mix together until combined.

Heat oil / lard in a pan and fry thinly spread pancakes until golden brown on both sides.

Serve immediately topped with sour cream and sugar.

Anna's note:

A blend of wild mushrooms is best: porcini, bolete, oyster mushrooms, portobello.
IMPORTANT: do not serve wild mushrooms to children.
Minced onion and bacon bits also make an awesome topping for this dish.

Sauerkraut & Mushroom Pierogi

— Pierogi z kapustą i grzybami —

Classic Polish dumplings filled with sauerkraut and wild mushrooms.

Yields: *100 dumplings*   **Prep time:** *1 hour*   **Cook time:** *5 minutes*

FILLING:

1 oz / 30 g of dried wild mushrooms*

1 large onion

8 oz / 250 g of portobello or button mushrooms

One 27 oz / 765 g can of sauerkraut

1 c / 235 ml of vegetable broth

¼ tsp black pepper

2 + 3 tbsp of butter

DOUGH:

6 c / 750 g of all-purpose flour

2 eggs

2 tsp of salt

2 ½ c / 600 ml of warm water

Pierogi freezing instructions on page 55!

To make the filling, you will need to soak dried mushrooms overnight or at least 4 hours. Then, boil in enough water to cover on low heat for about 20 minutes. Drain, but reserve the water from boiling. Cool and mince.

Heat 2 tablespoons of butter in a large frying pan on medium heat. Add minced onion. In the meantime, grate the portobello mushrooms on the largest vegetable grater and add to the pan. Sauté until golden brown. Add sauerkraut (liquid and all) to the pan, add wild mushrooms, vegetable broth, mushroom water, and pepper. Heat through and cook uncovered until all liquid evaporates (about 30 minutes). Add remaining butter, stir and cool. The filling is ready!

To make the dough, place egg and salt in bowl first, whisk lightly. Add flour and water. Mix until ingredients combine and form a dough ball. Transfer onto a floured surface and knead until smooth (3–4 minutes).

Cut away a portion and roll out with a rolling pin to about ⅛ inch / 2 millimeters in thickness. With a glass (or metal can or a pierogi cutter), cut out circles, place filling on each circle and close to form pierogi. When ready to boil, bring a large pot of salted water to boil then turn to low heat.

Place dumplings into the water in batches (7–10 at a time). Stir gently right away. When they float up to the top, let sit for about 2–3 minutes. Don't let the water roll: it may break your dumplings.

Remove from pot and spread on a large surface to cool (not touching), or serve right away. You can also brown them in a bit of butter until golden brown.

Yeast Apple Pancakes

— Racuchy —

*Fluffy pancakes
with apples cooked right into the batter.*

Yields: *20 pancakes*   **Prep time:** *10 minutes*   **Cook time:** *20 minutes*

2 tsp of instant yeast
1 ¾ c / 415 ml of warm milk
3 c / 375 g of all-purpose flour
2 tbsp of sugar
Pinch of salt
2 eggs
2 apples
3 tbsp of oil or lard
ADDITIONALLY:
Powdered sugar for garnish

Dissolve yeast in warm milk and let bloom for 10 minutes.

Combine flour with sugar and salt.

To milk, add the flour mixture and eggs. Mix until combined. Set aside in a warm place for at least 30 minutes.

Wash and peel apples. Cut into quarters, cut out the cores and thinly slice.

Add apples to dough and gently mix.

Heat oil in a non-stick pan. Pour dough into the pan to form pancakes.

Fry on both sides on medium-low heat until golden brown.

Sprinkle with powdered sugar before serving.

Meats & Poultry

Potrawy mięsne i drobiowe

Bacon Spread
— Smalec —

Slices of hearty bread, topped with aromatic "smalec", slices of sour pickles and onions is a popular but humble appetizer often served as a party starter.

Prep time: *15 minutes*   **Cook time:** *1–1.5 hours*

2 lbs / 1 kg of pork fat

½ lb / 250 g of raw pork belly

4 medium onions (about 2 c diced)

2 tart apples

10 garlic cloves, minced

½ tsp of freshly ground pepper

1 tsp salt

1 tbsp dried marjoram

¼ tsp caraway seed

Have your butcher coarse grind the pork fat, if possible. Dice pork belly. Set a large pot to medium heat and add just the pork fat. Render until all white is liquid and the bits start turning brown. This may take about 30–45 minutes.

Then, add pork belly and continue rendering until meat bits start browning, another 30 minutes or so.

In the meantime, dice onions and grate the apples. When meat bits are starting to brown, add onions and apples. Sauté until onions are nicely golden brown.

Finally, add minced garlic, pepper, salt, marjoram, and caraway seeds, stir well and cook for a couple of minutes.

Transfer to jars or decorative dishes and set aside to cool completely. Refrigerate. It will stay fresh in the fridge for weeks.

Anna's note:

Serve with crusty bread. Top with slices of pickles and / or fresh onions.

107

Beans & Sausage

– Fasolka po bretońsku –

Large, white beans, cooked with smoky sausage and tomato-based sauce. This filling fall dish can be served as a main meal. We often prepare it when cooking outside, or enjoy while camping.

Yields: *4–6 servings* **Prep time:** *10 minutes* **Cook time:** *20 minutes*

About ½ lb / 250 g of smoked sausage

½ lb / 250 g of smoked bacon

1 large onion

3–4 bay leaves

4–5 allspice berries, whole

One 29 oz / 822 g can of tomato puree / tomato sauce

2 tbsp of tomato paste

¼ tsp of salt

½ tsp of sugar

Two 15 oz / 439 g cans of white beans (great northern, navy beans or large lima beans)

Dice sausage and bacon and, in a large pan, sauté until golden around the edges. Add chopped onion, bay leaves, and allspice berries. Sauté until onion is golden brown.

Add tomato puree / sauce and tomato paste, salt, and sugar and simmer on low for about 10 minutes, uncovered, to reduce.

Drain and rinse beans. Add them to the mixture, stir, and heat through.

Taste. Add a bit more salt, if needed.

Anna's note:

I encourage you to use a good quality sausage and bacon that's smoky and not super fatty.

Beef Goulash

— Gulasz wołowy —

This classic thick and smooth sauce with beef chunks is often served with buckwheat and a side of pickle.

Yields: *4–5 servings*   **Prep time:** *10 minutes*   **Cook time:** *60–90 minutes*

About 1 lb / 500 g of stewing beef

½ tsp of salt

¼ tsp (or more) of ground pepper

3 tbsp of oil / grease

3 bay leaves

5 whole peppercorns and allspice berries (each)

1 onion

4 c / 1 l of broth (beef or chicken)

3 carrots

½ c / 120 ml of cold water

4 tbsp of all-purpose flour

Sprinkle beef with salt and pepper. In a medium saucepan, heat oil / grease, add beef, bay leaves, peppercorns and allspice berries.

Brown on high heat until edges start to brown, add chopped onion and sauté another few minutes, until onion cooks and browns a bit around the edges.

Add broth and simmer for about 45 minutes on medium-low.

Add cleaned, peeled and sliced carrots and simmer for another 15 minutes until beef reaches desired tenderness.

*In a small bowl, mix **cold** water with flour and whisk with a fork or a whisk. Add to sauce and bring to boil.*

Taste. Add more salt, if needed.

Anna's note:

Serve over favorite grain or other gravy soaker-upper.

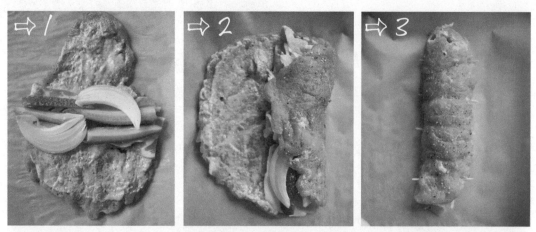

Beef Rolls

— Zrazy zawijane —

Tender beef steaks wrapped around smoky bacon and aromatic onions, cooked in sauce, best served over mashed potatoes.

Yields: *8 servings* **Prep time:** *20 minutes* **Cook time:** *45–60 minutes*

½ an onion

8 pickles

8 steaks (about 2.5 lbs / 1.2 kg of lean beef - eye round steak)

Salt and pepper

8 tbsp of brown mustard

8 oz / 250 g of smoked bacon

Toothpicks

Grease for sautéing

Another 1 ½ onions

1 qt / 1 l of beef or chicken stock

4 bay leaves

4–6 whole peppercorns and allspice berries (each)

3–4 dried mushrooms (if you have)

3 tbsp of all-purpose flour

½ c / 120 ml of cold water

Slice onion in half and then into thin wedges. Quarter each pickle.

Pound steaks out to about a pancake thickness. Sprinkle each one with salt and pepper and then spread about a tablespoon of mustard onto one side (thin layer–see pictures).

Cut bacon strips to fit the length of each steak and lay two pieces in the middle of each steak. Add pickles and onions.

Fold meat around the bacon / pickle / onion "stuffing". Fold the other end over the top, and secure the edges with toothpicks. Use as many as you need.

In a large frying pan, heat a thin layer of grease. Place rolls in single layer and sauté until golden brown on each side.

Take out rolls and add sliced 1 ½ onions. Sauté for about 5 minutes. Add rolls, beef / chicken stock, spices, and mushrooms and simmer on low for about 45 minutes. Take rolls and spices out and blend sauce with an immersion blender. Thicken the sauce by mixing flour and cold water and adding to the sauce. Bring to boil.

Taste. Add more salt, if needed.

Anna's note:

Make sure to remove toothpicks before serving.

"Kaszanka" Sandwich

Fried with Onions

Roasted "Kaszanka"

Blood Sausage 3 Ways

— Kaszanka na trzy sposoby —

Traditional Polish sausage prepared with pork, organ meat, blood, and buckwheat or pear barley. It should be quite peppery and aromatic.

— "Kaszanka" Sandwich —

"Kaszanka" (blood sausage)

Hearty bread with thick crust

Raw onions

Mustard and / or horseradish

Take "kaszanka" out of the natural casing. Slice and place on buttered bread.

Top with sliced raw onions, mustard, and / or horse-radish.

— Fried with Onions —

5–6 "kaszanka" links or 1 large round "kaszanka"

7–8 medium onions, sliced

3 tbsp of vegetable oil

3 tbsp of butter

Salt and pepper to taste

Slice onions and sauté in oil and butter until caramelized.

Remove blood sausage from casings, slice and add to onions. Mix until sausage breaks up and onions are somewhat combined with the mixture. Let it caramelize for a few minutes before mixing again. Stir and let caramelize again.

Enjoy on bread or with a side of fried egg. Mustard and horseradish are also great condiments that will complement the dish.

— Roasted "Kaszanka" —

5–6 "kaszanka" links

5–6 onions (1 small-medium onion per link)

2–3 tbsp of vegetable oil + 2 tbsp of butter

Salt and pepper (as much as you like)

Heat oven to 350°F / 180°C.

Slice onions and set aside.

Place oil and butter in a roasting pan and place in the oven for a couple of minutes to warm the oil and melt the butter. When butter is melted, add the onions, sprinkle with salt and pepper and mix to combine. Add the "kaszanka" links and roast for another 20–30 minutes.

Enjoy with mustard and / or horseradish and bread or potatoes for a full meal.

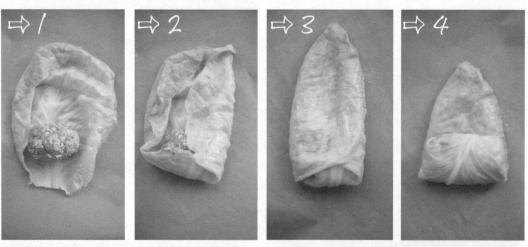

Cabbage Rolls

—Gołąbki—

Mixture of rice, pork, and beef rolled into a cabbage leaf, served with tomato or mushroom sauce.

Yields: *15 rolls* **Prep time:** *30 minutes* **Cook time:** *45 minutes*

2 ½ c of cooked rice

2 medium onions

2 tbsp / 25 g of butter

1 head of cabbage

½ lb / 250 g of ground beef

½ lb / 250 g of ground pork or turkey

1 tsp of salt

½ tsp of pepper

1 qt / 1 l of chicken or vegetable stock

3 bay leaves

Cook rice following the directions on the package, but shorten the cooking time by half. Sauté onions in butter.

Wash cabbage and cut out the core. Place cabbage in a pot (core down) and fill with water to cover the whole head. Start heating the water, and as the leaves start loosening away from the head, remove from water (careful! Hot!). Set leaves aside, and also reserve those that may break while separating.

Lay out cooled leaves and, with a sharp knife, shave off the thick part of the main vein of each leaf so the leaves lay flat (there may be a slight curve in the leaf).

Place ground meat in a large mixing bowl, add cooked rice, sautéed onion, salt, pepper. Mix until combined.

Depending on the size of the leaf, place a ball of meat in the natural curve of each leaf. Start rolling from the bottom up, next fold the sides in, then complete the roll (as pictured). Set rolls aside until all done.

Choose cooking method:

BOILING METHOD: *place broken leaves on the bottom of the pot you boiled the cabbage in and layer cabbage rolls on top, placing each roll seam down. Cover with any leftover leaves.*

Fill the pot with chicken stock to cover the layered rolls. Add bay leaves. Boil on low for about 30 minutes.

BAKING METHOD: *place rolls in a baking dish, cover with broken up leaves. Carefully add a little bit of stock (about ⅓ of the depth of the dish). Bake at 350°F / 180°C for about 45 minutes.*

Serve with favorite sauce — see the next page.

Cabbage Rolls: Sauces

— Tomato Sauce —

Two 14.5 oz / 410 ml cans of diced / stewed tomatoes or tomato sauce

6 oz / 170 g of tomato paste

3 c / 750 ml of chicken or vegetable broth

½ tsp of salt

3 bay leaves

5 whole peppercorns and allspice berries (each)

⅓ c / 80 ml of heavy cream

4 tbsp / 50 g of butter

Blend tomatoes with tomato paste, broth, and salt. Transfer to a medium saucepan, add spices and simmer on medium-low for about 15–20 minutes.

Turn off, add heavy cream and butter. Taste, add salt, if needed.

— Mushroom Sauce —

½ c / 10 g of dried wild mushrooms

6 oz / 170 g of fresh mushrooms (crimini, shiitake, oyster mushrooms, button mushrooms)

½ an onion, chopped

2 tbsp / 25 g of butter

¼ tsp of salt

3 bay leaves

5 whole peppercorns and allspice berries (each)

4 c / 1 l of chicken or vegetable stock

⅔ c / 160 ml of heavy cream

3 tbsp of all-purpose flour

½ c / 120 ml of cold water

1 tsp of butter

Soak dried mushrooms for 30 minutes in about 1 cup hot water.

Wash fresh mushrooms and chop into smaller pieces. Sauté in butter with onions and salt until golden brown around the edges (about 10–12 minutes). Add water from soaking dried mushrooms along with stock, bay leaves, peppercorns and allspice berries. Chop reconstituted dried mushrooms and add to sauce. Simmer on low for about 20 minutes.

Add cream. Combine **cold** water with flour and whisk. Add to sauce and bring to boil. Sauce will thicken. Add butter to finish off the sauce. Taste. Add more salt, if needed.

Anna's note:

IMPORTANT: do not serve dishes prepared with wild mushrooms to children.

"Gołąbki" can be served on their own, covered with your favorite sauce, or with a side of potatoes.

Anna's note:

Best to use broth from homemade chicken soup "rosół", pg. 19.

Chicken Aspic

— Galareta z kurczaka —

Tender chicken pieces molded into gelatine, garnished with a boiled egg, carrot slices, and peas. This traditional dish is usually served during Polish Easter.

Yields: *3 molds / servings* **Prep time:** *20 minutes + time to set*

2 c / 500 ml of chicken stock*

Two 0.25 oz envelopes of unflavored gelatin (or enough for 500 ml of liquid)

1 hard-boiled egg

1 carrot from chicken stock, or boiled separately

¼ c of frozen sweet peas

1 c of cooked chicken, shredded

Lemon juice or vinegar

Heat up chicken stock lightly; must be warm but not hot. Add gelatin and stir to dissolve.

Use small bowls (or glasses, coffee cups, or plastic storage containers: something with wide rim that will allow you to remove gelatin mold once it's set) to create molds.

Place one slice of hard-boiled egg on the bottom of each container, add a couple of slices of boiled carrot and 6–10 peas. Top with shredded chicken.

Gently pour gelatin / stock mixture over meat only until the liquid reaches the top of the meat. Let set for about 15–20 minutes, then pour the rest of the liquid to fill the container. This will prevent the contents from floating up to the surface.

Let set in the fridge for at least 2 hours.

To remove from mold, run a warm butter knife inside the perimeter of the mold, then place on a plate upside down.

To serve, sprinkle with lemon juice (or white vinegar) and serve with bread. Prepared horseradish is also an excellent topping.

Chicken Pâté

— Pasztet z kurczaka —

Pâté is a result of Poles using all of their ingredients. Chicken pâté is often prepared from meat left over from making Sunday soup "rosół". We love it on sandwiches, garnished with pickles and raw onions. "Pasztet" will always be served at Easter.

Yields: *2 bread loaf pans*   **Prep time:** *2 hours*   **Cook time:** *1 hour*

1 whole chicken (boiled or roasted)*

2 carrots

1 parsnip or parsley root

20 oz / 500 g of chicken livers

2 tbsp of vegetable oil

2 medium onions

6 oz / 150 g of fresh crimini mushrooms or 1 portobello mushroom

4 strips / 150 g of good quality, thick-cut smoked bacon (raw)

10 garlic cloves

6 sprigs of parsley

6 sprigs of dill

2 c / 500 ml of chicken or vegetable stock

3 eggs

Salt, pepper

Time saving tip: use rotisserie chicken instead of roasting your own.

Cook the chicken by boiling or roasting.

To boil, place in a pot covered with water, add carrots, parsnip / parsley root, and 2 teaspoons of salt. Boil on low for 1–1 ½ hours. Remove meat and veggies from stock and cool (reserve stock).

To roast, sprinkle chicken with a bit of salt, and pepper and place in a 350°F / 180°C oven. Roast until cooked (about 1 ½ hours), then cool (reserve juices from roasting).

Separate meat from bones.

Drain chicken livers and sauté in oil until fully cooked, set aside to cool. Chop onions and mushrooms and sauté in a bit of grease with a sprinkle of salt, set aside to cool. Cook carrots and parsnip (if they didn't cook with chicken), cool.

Put all ingredients (including chicken meat, livers, raw bacon, vegetables, garlic, parsley, and dill) through a meat grinder with the smallest grinding plate.

Preheat oven to 350°F / 180°C.

To the mixture, add 2 cups of stock or juice from roasting the chicken, salt to taste, and 1 teaspoon of black pepper. Mix and taste. Add a bit more salt, if needed. Add raw eggs. Mix well. Place in baking dishes. Bake for 1 hour, cool and refrigerate.

Serve cold, with hearty bread, garnished with sliced pickles and onions.

Chicken in Mushroom Sauce

−Kurczak w sosie grzybowym −

Tender chicken pieces in creamy mushroom sauce was always a hit in my home. Because it's such an easy recipe, it is often a go-to.

Yields: *2–4 servings* **Prep time:** *5 minutes* **Cook time:** *1 hour*

2 chicken legs; skin on (or 2 drumsticks and 2 thighs)

Salt and pepper

3 tbsp of oil

2 garlic cloves, crushed

1 large onion

8 oz / 250 g of button mushrooms (I like baby bellas)

2 tbsp of butter

2 c / 500 ml of water

5–6 whole peppercorns and allspice berries (each)

2 bay leaves

½ c / 120 ml of cold water

2 tbsp of all-purpose flour

Parsley for garnish

Sprinkle chicken legs with salt and pepper. Heat oil in a medium pan (or a dutch oven) and sear until golden brown, about 10 minutes (they don't have to be cooked through). Add crushed garlic while legs are searing.

In the meantime, chop onion and slice mushrooms. When chicken is seared, remove it and set aside.

To the same pan, add butter, onion, and mushrooms and sprinkle with salt. Sauté until juices flow and veggies cook a bit (about 10 minutes). Return meat to the pan, add water, peppercorns, allspice berries, and bay leaves, cover and simmer on low for about 45–60 minutes, or until meat is tender.

When meat is soft, combine water with flour, add to stew. Bring to boil to thicken.

Taste, add a bit of salt, if needed.

Serve over potatoes or dumplings, garnished with parsley.

Anna's note:

You can scale this recipe up or down. Remember to keep salt to meat ratio at 2 lbs to 1 tbsp of salt / 1 kg to 18 g of salt.

Fresh Sausage
– Biała kiełbasa –

Fresh pork sausage, with a distinct flavor of garlic and marjoram, prepared and served at Easter dinner alongside of "żurek".

Prep time: *1 hour*   **Cook time:** *20–30 minutes*

One 8 oz / 227 g package of natural 32 mm hog casings

8 lbs / 3 ½ kg of ground pork (shoulder or pork butt)

1 lb / 500 g of pork belly

6 garlic cloves, minced

4 tbsp / 72 g of fine sea or rock salt

1 tsp of freshly ground black pepper

1 c / 235 ml of ice-cold water

2 tbsp of dried marjoram

Soak and rinse the casings as directed on the package.

You can purchase pork shoulder whole and grind at home, or have your butcher grind it at the store. Pork belly will have to be ground up also. If you're grinding it at home, use the small grinding plate.

Place ground pork in a large container, add garlic, salt, pepper, water, and marjoram and massage with your hands for about 10 minutes.

Assemble sausage stuffer. Slide one casing on the sausage attachment fully, and feed the meat through the top of the hopper, filling each casing to the desired sausage length, twisting after each link.

If you're using a kitchen mixer with a sausage attachement, turn the mixer to high; it will make it easier for the meat to go through. Leave a few inches of unfilled casing at the beginning and at the end of each casing, to prevent spilling. You can also tie the end off if you so choose. The meat should be packed pretty well, but careful with overfilling; the casings may break. Don't puncture casings at any point.

Consume within 2 days or freeze to store. Make sure to defrost in the fridge.

Enjoy with sour rye soup (pg. 45) or boiled (boil on low heat for 20–30 minutes). You can also grill or roast in the oven.

Fried Pork Cutlets

— Kotlet schabowy —

Thin pork cutlets, breaded and pan fried, are a staple of Polish cooking. This favorite dinner is one of the most-loved Polish dishes of all time.

Yields: *6 cutlets* **Prep time:** *10 minutes* **Cook time:** *20 minutes*

About 1 lb / 500 g of boneless pork loin

Salt & pepper

2 large eggs

¾ c / 135 g of bread crumbs

About ⅓ c of pork lard for frying

ADDITIONALLY:

Meat tenderizer

Slice pork loin into 6 thick slices. Pound each slice to about ¼ inch / 0.5 cm thickness. I like my pork chops relatively small, so after pounding it out, I cut each one in half. Sprinkle each cutlet with salt and pepper on each side.

Break eggs into a shallow bowl and whisk with a fork. Place bread crumbs in another shallow bowl.

Heat about 3 tablespoons of pork lard in a large pan. Dip each pork chop in the egg to cover, then in bread crumbs.

Fry for about 2–3 minutes on each side on medium heat, until golden brown.

Serve immediately with a side of boiled potatoes garnished with dill and a favorite Polish salad.

Anna's note:

I recommend cucumber salad (pg. 187) or cold beetroot salad (pg. 171).

Hunter's Stew

— Bigos —

Fresh cabbage and sauerkraut mixture, spiked with smoky sausage and bacon pieces, naturally sweetened with tomatoes and cooked for hours. This traditional dish is often served at gatherings, and it is a favorite party dish. We always had a big pot going in the basement kitchen.

Yields: *6–10 servings*   **Prep time:** *15 minutes*   **Cook time:** *2 hours*

1 ½ c of dried mushrooms + about 1 ½ c of water for soaking

About 1 lb / 500 g of beef and / or pork (or leftover roast)

2–3 tbsp of oil

6 strips of smoked bacon

1 large onion

8 oz / 225 g of fresh button mushrooms

1 small cabbage

About 1 lb / 500 g of smoked sausage, diced

1 c / 250 ml of chicken / beef / vegetable stock

6 oz / 170 g of tomato paste (or ⅓ c of ketchup or one 14 oz / 410 g can of stewed tomatoes)

3 tsp of salt

4–5 bay leaves

1 garlic clove

10 whole peppercorns and allspice berries (each)

½ tsp of ground pepper

About 56 oz / 1.5 kg of sauerkraut

Soak dried mushrooms for about 1 hour. When soft, chop (reserve water from soaking).

If using raw meat, cut into bite size pieces, sprinkle with salt and pepper. In a large pot (4–5 quart), heat oil and sear meat.

Remove meat from pan, add cubed bacon and render for a few minutes. Add onion and sliced fresh mushrooms. Sauté until golden brown, for about 3 minutes. In the meantime, thinly slice fresh cabbage.

When onions and mushrooms are cooked, add fresh cabbage to the pot, return the cooked beef / pork, and add chopped dried mushrooms. Add diced sausage and stock, tomato paste, salt (about 2 teaspoons) bay leaves, garlic, peppercorns, allspice berries, ground pepper and mix.

Cover and cook on medium to medium-low heat for about 15 minutes (until cabbage is soft). Stir occasionally.

Add sauerkraut, mix, cover and cook for another 1.5 hours. Best if cooked again (for about 1 hour) the next day.

Anna's note:

This dish can alternatively be prepared with wild game or without any meat at all.

Meatballs

—Pulpety—

Comforting dish of smooth sauce, best when served over mashed potatoes. Kids of all ages love this one.

Yields: *30 meatballs* **Prep time:** *15 minutes* **Cook time:** *45 minutes*

1 onion

2 tbsp of butter

About 1 lb / 500 g of beef

About 1 lb / 500 g of pork (pork loin or shoulder, but any part will do)

4 garlic cloves

1 boiled carrot (optional)

4 slices of bread or ½ cup of bread crumbs or 2 dinner rolls

2 tbsp of minced parsley

1 raw egg

½ tbsp of salt

½ tsp of ground pepper

4 c / 1 l of broth (chicken, beef or vegetable)

4 bay leaves

6–8 whole peppercorns and allspice berries (each)

6 slices of dried mushrooms

¾ c / 180 ml of cold water

3 tbsp of all-purpose flour

Mince onion and sauté in butter until golden brown around the edges.

Cube meat and put through a meat grinder, follow with garlic, carrot, and bread slices (if using bread).

To meat mixture, add sautéd onion, parsley, egg, bread crumbs (if using instead of bread), salt, pepper. Mix until combined.

Heat broth in a medium pot with bay leaves, peppercorns, allspice berries, and mushrooms. Form even balls (I like using an ice-cream scoop; the balls come out the same size) about 2 inches / 5 centimeters in diameter. Drop raw balls into simmering broth (over low heat).

Simmer for 15 minutes. Take one out, cut open and see if it's cooked.

When cooked through, take meatballs out and strain the sauce though a small strainer.

In a small bowl, whisk cold water and flour. Return broth to pot and heat through. Add water / flour mixture to thicken the sauce. Bring to boil. Taste. Amount of salt will depend on your broth, so if you think it needs more, add a bit at a time.

Return meatballs to the sauce and heat before serving. Garnish with parsley.

Kids love this!

Anna's note:

Leftover patties can be sliced and served on bread, as a sandwich topping for breakfast or lunch.

Minced Meat Cutlets

– Kotlety mielone –

Minced meat cutlets similar to American burgers. This is yet another favorite that will never be turned down by anyone, not even a picky eater.

Yields: *10 cutlets*   **Prep time:** *15 minutes*   **Cook time:** *20 minutes*

1 carrot

½ an onion

2 tbsp of butter

About 1 lb / 500 g of ground meat mixture (pork & beef, beef & veal, or beef & turkey)

1 tbsp of chopped parsley

½ tsp of salt

¼ tsp of ground pepper

1 egg

2 tbsp of bread crumbs

Oil for frying

Wash and peel the carrot, slice and boil until soft (or if you have one left over from Sunday "rosół", use that; just mash with a fork). When carrot is soft, mash with a fork and set aside.

Dice onion and sauté in butter until golden brown.

Place all ingredients (including carrot and sautéd onion) in a mixing bowl and mix until combined.

When ready to form meat patties, wet your hands (so meat won't stick) and grab even amounts of meat and roll into a ball (I like to use a ⅓ cup ice-cream scoop for this, but that's quite small for most, so consider making them larger). Once a ball is formed, flatten the ball to create a patty.

Heat a couple of tablespoons of grease in a frying pan and place patties in the pan.

Brown over medium heat for about 5 minutes on each side, or until cooked through.

Serve hot, accompanied by a steaming pile of potatoes garnished with dill, and a favorite fresh salad (I think a carrot salad is perfect for it, see pg. 181).

Pork Aspic

— Studzienina / Zimne nogi —

This old dish is still prepared and served in Poland. My family eats it only once every year, during Easter. It is savory, aromatic and quite tasty.

Yields: *2 loaf pans* **Prep time:** *4 hours + cooling*

- 2 pig's feet (about 2 lbs / 1 kg)
- About 2 lbs / 1 kg of raw ham hocks
- 8 c / 2 l of water
- 2–3 carrots
- 1 parsnip or parsley root
- ¼ of a celery root
- 1 medium onion (burnt over gas burner or in a dry frying pan)
- 10 whole peppercorns and all-spice berries (each)
- 4–5 bay leaves
- 2 tsp + ½ tsp of salt
- 4 garlic cloves, crushed + 5 garlic cloves, minced
- 1 tsp of ground pepper
- ½ tsp of dried marjoram

Wash all pork and place in a large stock pot with water, carrots, parsnip / parsley root, celery root, onion, peppercorns, allspice berries, bay leaves, 2 teaspoons of salt, and 4 crushed garlic cloves. Bring to boil, turn heat to low and simmer for 1 hour.

Take out vegetables and continue simmering for another 2–3 hours, or until meat is tender and falling off the bone.

After meat is cooked, remove it from stock and set aside until cool enough to manage.

In the meantime, strain stock, slice vegetables and mince garlic. Return sliced vegetables and add garlic, pepper, and marjoram to stock. Taste. Add a bit more salt, if needed.

Once meat has cooled off, take off the bone and remove some of the fat. Slice meat, skin and return to stock.

Pour into containers. Cool at room temperature and then transfer to the fridge.

To serve, cut into thick slices.

Anna's note:

Enjoy with bread, garnished with vinegar or lemon juice and / or horseradish.

Pork Ribs with Sauerkraut

—Żeberka w kapuście—

Filling one-pot meal of sauerkraut and pork ribs makes a great fall or winter dinner. Serve with potatoes or just a side of hearty bread.

Yields: *3–4 servings*   **Prep time:** *15 minutes*   **Cook time:** *2 hours*

1.5 lbs / 700 g of pork ribs

Salt and pepper

6 oz / 170 g of thick-cut smoked bacon

2 small onions

3 garlic cloves

3 tbsp of cooking oil

3 tbsp of all-purpose flour

2 c / 500 ml of chicken or vegetable stock

Two 14.5 oz cans / about 1 kg of sauerkraut*

½ tsp of fresh thyme

5–6 whole peppercorns and allspice berries (each)

3 bay leaves

Wash and dry ribs. Cut into 1 bone sections. Sprinkle with salt and pepper and set aside. Cut bacon into cubes, chop onion and peel and mince garlic.

Pre-heat oven to 350°F / 180°C.

In a medium / large pan, heat oil. Add ribs and cook until golden brown on both sides (about 10 minutes per side), remove from heat and set aside. Into the same pan, add bacon, onion, and garlic and sauté. When onion and bacon are golden brown, add flour and chicken / vegetable stock. Whisk to combine. Add sauerkraut, thyme, peppercorns, allspice berries, and bay leaves. Mix well and heat through.

In a large baking dish, place half of the sauerkraut mixture, then a layer of ribs and then sauerkraut again. Bake covered for 2 hours. Check after about 1.5 hours of cooking to make sure there is a bit of moisture left; if not, add a few tablespoons of water or stock.

Serve with hearty bread or boiled potatoes.

Anna's note:

Consider rinsing sauerkraut before cooking if you don't like it too sour. Personally, I like it sour!

Roasted Duck

— Kaczka pieczona —

Poles love celebrating special occasions with food. Roasted duck paired with Silesian dumplings "kluski śląskie" and sweet and sour red cabbage with apples or raspberries often fits the bill. It will be served several times every year, especially in early fall season.

Yields: *5–6 servings* **Prep time:** *20 minutes* **Cook time:** *2.5–3 hours*

1 duck

1 tbsp of salt

2 tsp of freshly ground pepper

1 tbsp of dried marjoram

STUFFING:

10 oz / 30 g of chicken and / or duck livers

10 oz / 30 g of chicken and / or duck gizzards

1 kaiser roll

3 whole eggs

4 oz / 100 g of butter

3 tbsp of fresh parsley

2 tsp of salt

2 tsp of pepper

ADDITIONALLY:

Needle and a natural thread for sewing up the duck

Rinse duck and pat dry. Sprinkle with salt, pepper, and marjoram. Leave out of the fridge to bring to room temperature.

Rinse livers and gizzards, set aside to drain. Place kaiser roll in a container with a cup of water, let it soak it up.

Put livers and gizzards through a meat grinder; at the end, squeeze water out of the kaiser roll and also put through the grinder.

To the stuffing mixture, add eggs, diced butter, chopped parsley, salt, and pepper and mix until well combined.

Preheat oven to 350°F / 180°C

Prepare needle and thread. Place duck in a baking dish. Spoon stuffing into the duck, filling as much as you can. Fold ducktail up and sew up with the needle and thread to close the cavity and keep the stuffing from flowing out.

***Cover** baking dish and bake 2.5–3 hours (about 30 minutes per pound / about 1 hour per kilo).*

Baste with juices that duck produces about once every hour. Take cover off for the last 20 minutes and let the bird brown.

Rest for 10–15 minutes before serving.

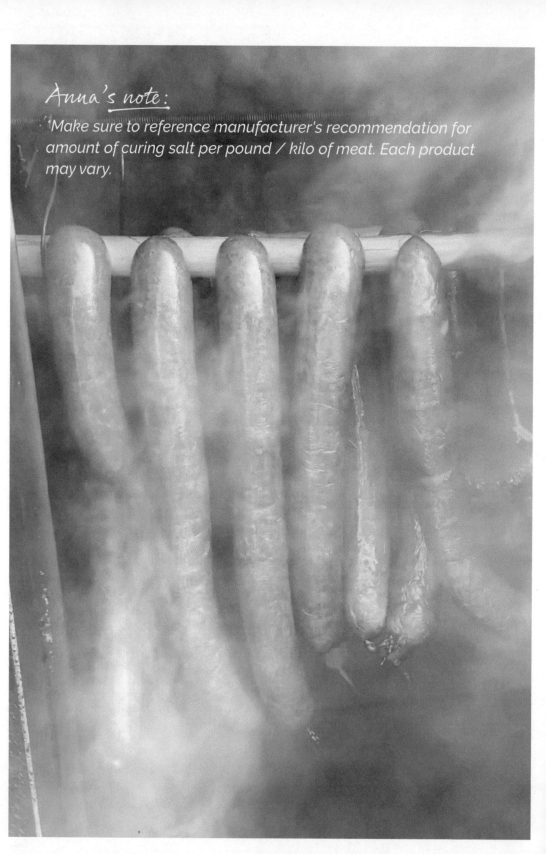

Anna's note:
*Make sure to reference manufacturer's recommendation for amount of curing salt per pound / kilo of meat. Each product may vary.

Smoked Sausage

—Kiełbasa wędzona—

This is a basic recipe for smoked sausage, but varieties are endless here in Poland. Start here and explore other flavors by adding a bit of your own touch to it. I like mine basic, like this: garlicky and peppery, on the leaner side.

Prep time: *1 hour + resting*   **Cook time:** *6 hours + cooling*

One 8 oz / 227 g package of natural 32 mm hog casings

9 lbs / 4 kg of pork (shoulder or butt)

2 lbs / 1 kg of pork belly or pork fat

1 qt / 1 l of water

5 tbsp / 80 g of fine sea or rock salt

1 tsp curing salt*

5 tbsp of ground pepper

5–10 garlic cloves

Grind pork (shoulder / butt) using the largest-opening grinding plate. Grind pork belly / fat using the smallest grinding plate.

Place ground meat in a large container, add water, salt, curing salt, and pepper and massage with your hands until sticky (about 10–15 minutes). Refrigerate for 24 hours.

When ready to stuff, add crushed garlic and massage again until well combined.

Stuff into casings tightly, separating into desired links.

Hang to dry for 2 hours in cool, well-ventilated room.

Smoke at 120–140°F / 50–60°C for 3 hours, then parboil at 170°F / 75°C for 20 minutes.

Hang dry in well-ventilated room until cool.

Refrigerate laid out or loosely wrapped in parchment paper until ready to eat.

Enjoy sliced on sandwiches, grilled, oven roasted with onions, or over a fire.

Homemade "kiełbasa" will keep in the fridge, loosely wrapped in paper, for 3 – 4 weeks.

Stewed Pork Ribs

— Żeberka w sosie —

Soft, fall-off-the-bone ribs in thick sauce will surprise with flavor and texture. I love them with drop dumplings and a side of hot fried beets.

Yields: *3–4 servings* **Prep time:** *15 minutes* **Cook time:** *1.5 hours*

1 rack (about 2 lbs / 1 kg) of baby back ribs

Pinch of salt and pepper

2 tbsp of oil

4 garlic cloves

6-ish sprigs of thyme

6 c / 1.5 l of water (or stock)

5–6 slices of dried mushroom

¼ of an onion (burnt over gas burner or in a dry frying pan)

5–7 whole peppercorns and allspice berries (each)

1 carrot

1 stick of celery

4 tbsp of all-purpose flour

½ c / 120 ml of cold water

Wash and dry ribs. Cut into sections of 2 ribs each. Sprinkle with salt and pepper.

Heat oil in a large pot. Add ribs and sauté on each side (about 8–10 minutes total). About halfway through sautéing, add crushed garlic and a few sprigs of thyme.

When golden on the edges, add water (or stock) to cover meat. Add mushroom slices, onion, allspice berries, peppercorns, carrot, and celery.

When water starts boiling, turn heat to low and simmer for 1.5 hours (or until meat is soft and falls off the bone).

Gently take meat and veggies out of the pot.

Whisk flour with cold water and add to sauce. Bring to boil.

Taste and add salt, if needed, and a generous sprinkle of freshly ground pepper.

Serve over potatoes or favorite dumplings.

Turkey Steaks with Horseradish Cream Sauce

— Indyk w sosie chrzanowym —

The cooking method will make the turkey tender, and the smooth and slightly spicy sauce gives this mild meat a nice "punch". The sauce is not super spicy, but this will depend on the spice level of your horseradish.

Yields: *4–6 servings* **Prep time:** *10 minutes* **Cook time:** *1 hour*

- 1.5 lbs / 650 g of turkey (chicken breast, pork loin, pork shoulder or veal chops can also be used)
- Salt and ground pepper
- 1–2 tbsp of vegetable oil
- ½ a medium onion, chopped
- 4 c / 1 l of water
- 6–8 whole peppercorns and allspice berries (each)
- 2 bay leaves
- 2 tbsp of butter
- 3 tbsp of all-purpose flour
- ¾ c / 180 ml of sweet cream
- ¾ c / 190 g of prepared horseradish
- ½ tsp of sugar
- 1 tsp of lemon juice

Whatever meat you are using, prepare by slicing into ¾ inch / 2 centimeter slices / cutlets. Sprinkle each piece with a bit of salt and pepper.

In a deep sautéing pan, heat vegetable oil. Add meat and sauté for 2–3 minutes on each side, until golden brown. Meat doesn't have to be cooked through; it will finish cooking in the sauce.

Once all of your meat is browned, remove from the pan and to pan add chopped onion and sauté for a couple of minutes. Once a bit brown around the edges, return meat to the pan, add water, peppercorns, allspice berries, and bay leaves and bring to boil. Turn heat to low and simmer until meat is soft (turkey - about 30 minutes; pork will take a bit longer - about 45 minutes).

Once meat is soft, gently remove from liquid. Also remove peppercorns, allspice berries and bay leaves.

*In a small sautéing pan, heat butter until melted, add flour and whisk until combined. **Slowly** start adding cream and continue whisking vigorously to prevent clumps. Turn heat off, add horseradish and continue whisking until completely combined. Add a bit of broth from sauce and whisk.*

Finally, transfer horseradish mixture to the sauce. Add lemon juice, sugar and a bit more salt and freshly ground pepper. Also return the meat to sauce and bring to boil. Taste and add more salt and pepper, if needed.

Perfect with drop dumplings — recipe on page 65.

Toasted Sandwiches

—Zapiekanki—

Street food of many Polish cities, "zapiekanki" can also be prepared and enjoyed at home. Basic baguette-type bread is topped with mushrooms and cheese and other toppings of choice. This recipe features four popular varieties, prepared at the same time.

16 oz / 500 g of button mushrooms

2–3 tbsp of butter

Salt and pepper

14 oz / 400 g of cheese (Gouda, Pepper Jack, Muenster cheese or Swiss)

1 baguette (about 80 cm / 30 inches)

Clean and slice mushrooms. Preheat a large pan, add butter and sliced mushrooms. Sprinkle with a bit of salt and pepper. Sauté on medium heat until all moisture cooks off. In the meantime, shred cheese and also sauté bacon for bacon & jalapeno "zapiekanka" until almost done (it will get a bit more crispy in the oven). Set aside.

Preheat oven to 350°F / 180°C.

Cut baguette in half (in length) and each half along the side to create open-faced sandwiches. Lay out on a parchment-lined baking dish. Divide mushrooms into four parts and top each piece of baguette with mushrooms and then cheese.

— Bacon & Jalapeno "Zapiekanka" —

4–6 slices of smoked bacon

1 fresh jalapeno (or a few slices of pickled jalapeno)

Garlic sauce (see the next page)

Top one piece of baguette with bacon.

—Ham & French-fried Onion "Zapiekanka" —

4–6 slices of smoked ham

Ketchup

A few tablespoons of French-fried onions

Top one piece of baguette with ham.

— Sausage & Pickle "Zapiekanka" —

About 3 inch / 8 cm piece of smoked sausage, sliced

½ a small onion, white or red, thinly sliced

2 medium pickles, sliced

A pinch of red pepper flakes (optional)

Ketchup

Top one piece of baguette with sausage slices and onions.

— Ketchup & Green Onion "Zapiekanka" —

Ketchup

Green onions, chopped

The last piece of baguette will only have mushrooms and cheese toppings when baking.

— Next Steps —

Bake all 4 "zapiekanki" until crispy on top (about 5 minutes). In the meantime, prepare garlic sauce (recipe below).

Take out and top each piece of baguette with the remaining ingredients.

—Homemade Garlic Sauce—

4 tbsp of plain yogurt / Greek yogurt / sour cream

1 tbsp of mayonnaise

1 garlic clove, minced

A pinch of salt

A pinch of sugar

A pinch of ground black pepper

A good squirt of lemon juice

Mix together.

Anna's note:

Optionally, you are free to use hoagie rolls, Kaiser rolls, or shorter baguettes. Also, feel free to experiment with other toppings!

Fish

Ryby

Christmas Carp

— Karp bożonarodzeniowy —

Carp is a go-to fish served on most Polish Christmas Eve dinner tables. The flavor is quite unique, the meat tender and flaky. It is served only once every year and I cannot imagine Christmas without it.

Prep time: *2 hours*   **Cook time:** *20 minutes*

Whole carp - about 2 lbs/ 1 kg (if you can't find carp, striped bass is a nice substitute)

2 tbsp of salt

½ tsp of ground pepper

4 tbsp of flour

3 tbsp of oil

2 tbsp of butter

Clean and wash fish. Cut head, tail, and fins off. Cut fish into steaks.

Place fish in a bowl, add salt, cover with cold water and refrigerate for 2 hours. Remove, rinse and pat dry.

Sprinkle with pepper. Place flour in a shallow dish. Place each piece in flour to cover. Shake off any excess flour.

In a large frying pan, heat oil and butter. Place pieces of fish and sauté for a few minutes on each side on medium heat. Remove and place on a paper towel to soak up extra fat. If steaks are thick, finish in a 350°F / 180° C oven.

Serve immediately or keep in a warm oven until ready to serve.

Anna's note:

Pasteurized jars can be stored unrefrigerated and will keep for up to 6 months. Alternatively, you can place hot spread in jars, seal with the lid and refrigerate for up to 7 days.

Fish & Rice Sandwich Spread

– Paprykarz szczeciński –

"Paprykarz szczeciński" is an iconic symbol of the West Pomeranian region of Poland, and the city of Szczecin, where I'm from. It became famous in the 60s, developed by a local deep-sea fishing company to utilize all fish parts in their production process. It was inspired by the company's African journeys, and quickly became a favorite. It is quite popular nationwide; we mostly enjoy it on sandwiches.

Yields: *Eight 8 oz / 220 ml jars*   **Prep time:** *20 minutes*   **Cook time:** *20 minutes + pasteurizing*

½ cup / 100 g of uncooked rice

1 lb / 500 g of fish fillets (I'm using cod, but any kind of fish would do)

Pinch of salt and pepper

3 medium onions

3 tbsp of butter

2 bay leaves

3–4 allspice berries

3 carrots

26 oz / 750 g of diced tomatoes (canned)

1 tsp of paprika

ADDITIONALLY:

Eight 8 oz / 220 ml canning jars

Cook rice in salted water and set aside.

Cook fish, sprinkled with a bit of salt and pepper, in a little grease. Set aside to cool a bit. Once cool, break up with a fork until pretty fine.

Dice onions and sauté in a large pot in a bit of butter for about 5 minutes on medium-high heat with bay leaves and allspice berries. Wash, peel and grate carrots on the largest side of a box grater, add to onions and sauté for another 5 minutes.

Add tomatoes and heat through. Add paprika, rice, fish, freshly ground pepper (about ¼ teaspoon) and salt to taste (about a teaspoon). Mix well.

This recipe makes quite a bit, so I place it in jars and pull one out when I'm ready to eat. To do so, sanitize your jars and lids, place mixture into jars while still warm, place lids on and cool. Place in a shallow pot and fill with water just bellow the lid. Boil for 60 minutes. Take out and cool (unrefrigerated). After 24 hours repeat the process, but boil for 40 minutes. After another 24 hours repeat the process but boil for 30 minutes only.

I like this dish cold, so I place one jar in the fridge and store until cooled.

Serve cold, on bread.

Greek-style Fish

— Ryba po grecku —

"Ryba po grecku" is a dish that is mostly served during Polish Christmas Eve dinner, when Poles obey a strict no-meat rule. Even though the name may suggest that this dish came to us from Greece, it is actually an original dish to Poland. It is always present on my Christmas table.

Yields: *5–6 servings*   **Prep time:** *10 minutes*   **Cook time:** *30 minutes*

1 lb / 500 g of fish fillets (any white, mild fish will do)

1 egg

3 tbsp of all-purpose flour

3–4 tbsp of oil

5 carrots

1 parsnip

½ a medium celery root or ¾ of a small one

1 ½ c of chopped onion

1 tbsp of oil + 1 tbsp of butter

6 whole peppercorns and all-spice berries (each)

3 bay leaves

½ c / 110 ml of vegetable broth or water

3 tbsp of tomato paste

1 tsp salt

Sprinkle of pepper

2 tsp paprika

Wash fish fillets, pat dry and cut into about 3–4 inch / 8–10 centimeter pieces. Sprinkle with salt and pepper.

Break an egg into one dish, add a tablespoon of water and scramble. Place flour in another dish. Heat oil in a non-stick frying pan. Dip each piece of fish in egg, then flour and sauté on medium until cooked and lightly golden brown. Remove and place on a paper towel.

Peel carrots, parsnip, and celery root and grate on the largest side of a vegetable box grater. Chop onion. Heat oil and butter in a wide pan / deep frying pan and add peppercorns, allspice berries, and bay leaves, followed by shredded vegetables and onions. Heat through. Add broth, tomato paste, salt and pepper, and paprika. Sauté until cooked, about 5–7 minutes. Don't overcook; leave a bit of crunch in the veggies.

Taste. Add a bit more salt, if needed.

Once veggies are cooked, create layers in a serving dish by placing about ⅓ of the veggie mixture first, then arrange fish pieces and cover with the rest of the veggie mixture. Cover with foil and let cool.

Refrigerate until serving.

Herring in Oil

— Śledź w oleju —

Herring is one of Poland's favorite party dishes. There are many variations of the dish; this is the simplest one. If you are an adventurous eater, explore different options by experimenting with different ingredients. Try adding walnuts, cranberries, pickled mushrooms, or sun-dried tomatoes.

Yields: *4–5 small servings*   **Prep time:** *15 minutes + 2 hours for soaking*

8–9 oz / 225–250 g of herring fillets*

1 medium to large onion

1 c / 235 ml of vegetable oil (I like canola or flaxseed oil)

¼ tsp of black pepper (freshly ground, if possible)

½ c of chopped parsley

Place herring in a large bowl with a quart / liter of cold water and let soak for 2 hours. Change water out every 30 minutes.

Take out and set on paper towels to dry a bit.

Cut onion in half and slice thinly. Place in a bowl.

To onion add oil, pepper, and chopped parsley.

Slice herring at an angle into about 1 inch / 3 centimeter strips. Add to bowl with onions.

Mix and refrigerate until serving. Best if prepared 2–3 days ahead of time.

Serve with hearty rye bread.

Store in the fridge for up to 14 days, if needed.

Anna's note:

* Salted (not pickled) herring called "herring a la Matias" will work best.

Herring in Sour Cream
– Śledź w śmietanie –

Herring in sour cream is a very interesting dish as it plays on our senses by combining salty and sweet, cold and hot. It has a reserved spot on my family's Christmas Eve table every year. It is a traditional flavor of Polish holidays.

Yields: *3–4 small servings*   **Prep time:** *15 minutes + 2 hours for soaking*

About 7 oz / 200 g of herring fillets*

1 large onion

1 apple

1 c / 235 ml of sour cream

3–5 medium potatoes

Pinch of pepper

Place herring in a large bowl with a quart / liter of cold water and let soak for 2 hours. Change water out every 30 minutes.

In the meantime, cut the onion in half and thinly slice each half (or use mandoline for even slices). Place slices in a strainer and run about a quart / liter of freshly boiled water through the onions to slightly soften them and take the sharpness away.

Drain the herring and pat dry. Cut into bite-sized pieces. Place in a mixing bowl.

Once the onions have cooled, grate the apple on the largest side of a box grater and add both to the fish.

Add sour cream immediately, to prevent the apple from turning brown. Add pepper and mix well.

Cover and cool in the fridge for at least an hour.

When ready to serve, boil peeled potatoes in salted water. Place hot potatoes on a plate and top with the cold fish mixture.

Anna's note:

* *Salted (not pickled) herring called "herring a la Matias" will work best.*

Anna's note:

*Salted (not pickled) herring called "herring a la Matias" will work best. To enjoy this salad properly, one must reach through all layers and scoop out a serving. Herring is rather salty, so use judgement before adding more salt.

Layered Herring Salad

—Śledź pod pierzynką—

The name of this salad in Polish translates to "herring under a feather blanket".
The layers of the salad are prepared so as to create a soft texture,
with flavors harmoniously blended when consumed.

Yields: *10–12 servings*   **Prep time:** *45 minutes*

16 oz / 460 g of herring fillets*
3 medium potatoes
3 medium carrots
5 eggs
1 c / 235 ml of mayonnaise
Parsley or dill
Salt and pepper

Place herring in a large bowl with a quart / liter of cold water and let soak for 2 hours. Change water out every 30 minutes. Once done, place on paper towels and pat dry. Mince fillets and set aside.

Wash potatoes and peel carrots. Boil both (together is fine) in salted water until soft, then cool completely. Once cool, peel potatoes and set aside until ready to assemble the layers. Hard boil eggs, set aside to cool.

In a glass dish (with a wide bottom so you can see the layers–I'm using a 7 cup / 1650 ml dish), place minced herring on the bottom and spread evenly with the back of a spoon. Sprinkle with pepper. Next, with the back of a spoon spread 1 tablespoon of mayonnaise over the layer of herring.

Next, on the largest side of a box grater, grate potatoes over the herring layer and gently spread evenly. Add 1 tablespoon of mayonnaise on the top of potato layer and, with the back of a spoon, spread it evenly. Sprinkle with a bit of pepper and about a tablespoon of minced parsley.

Next layer will be carrots. On the largest side of a box grater, grate carrots over potato layer and spread evenly. Add 1 tablespoon of mayonnaise to the top and, with the back of a spoon, spread it evenly. Sprinkle with a bit of pepper and about a tablespoon of minced parsley.

Next layer is the egg layer. Peel eggs and grate over the carrot layer. As with the layers before, cover with a layer of mayo. Lastly, sprinkle with parsley.

This layered salad will not be mixed. Chill until ready to serve.

Salmon Spread
– Pasta rybna <u>tososiowa</u> –

This is an updated version of a fish spread that we used to (and still can) purchase in a metal tube. This more aromatic homemade rendition surpasses the flavor of anything purchased at a grocery store.

Yields: *1 cup*   **Prep time:** *15 minutes*

7 oz / 200 g piece of raw salmon
1 tsp of butter
2 tbsp of ketchup
4 oz / 120 g of cream cheese
2 garlic cloves
1 tsp of minced onion
1 tsp of fresh dill
Salt & pepper

Sprinkle raw fish with salt and pepper and sauté in butter until cooked through (about 7–10 minutes). It's also okay to use fish that's already been cooked or grilled–we love leftovers! Remove cooked fish from the pan and let cool.

Once fish is cold, place in a food processor with ketchup, cream cheese, and garlic (or use an immersion blender) and blend into a smooth paste.

Once blended, add finely minced onion and chopped dill. Mix with a spoon or a spatula (but don't blend).

Taste. It will most likely need a bit more salt, but this will depend on the saltiness of the fish. Add more salt, if needed, and a pinch of pepper. Mix well and refrigerate until serving.

Serve chilled with bread or favorite crackers.

This is a great party dish!

Vegetables

Warzywa

Beetroot Salad

— Surówka z buraków —

Salad made from roasted beets, with the addition of sharp, fresh onion, lemon, and spices. It makes a great side dish to saucy meat dishes.

Yields: *4 servings*   **Prep time:** *10 minutes + 1.5 hours for roasting beets*

3 medium beets
¼ of a small onion
1 tsp of oil
Juice of ½ of a large lemon
Pinch of salt
½ tsp of sugar
½ tsp white vinegar

Preheat oven to 350°F / 180°C. Cut stems off beets and scrub to clean.

Bake covered for about 1 hour or until soft. Take out and set aside to cool.

Once cooled off, peel and grate on the largest side of a box grater. Add chopped onion, oil, lemon juice, salt, sugar, and vinegar. Mix and refrigerate to cool.

Buckwheat & Mushroom Cabbage Rolls

– Gołąbki z kaszą gryczaną i grzybami –

*Vegetarian filling of earthy buckwheat and mushrooms,
rolled in soft cabbage leaves.*

Yields: *14–15 rolls* **Prep time:** *60–90 minutes* **Cook time:** *45 minutes*

1 large savoy cabbage

FILLING:

1 ½ c / 250 g of uncooked buckwheat

1 ½ c of diced onion (½ a large onion)

10 oz / 280 g of button mushrooms

2 tbsp / 30 g of butter

2 tsp of freshly ground pepper

2 tbsp of fresh thyme

1 tsp of salt

1 tsp of granulated onion

1 garlic clove or 1 tsp of garlic powder

1 egg

To prepare cabbage, insert a small knife around the core to remove. Some leaves may be loose.

Place the head in a large pot, with water to cover about 75% of the head, core down. Heat covered until water starts boiling. Carefully observe outer leaves and, with tongs, remove one by one when they become softened and pliable to the point that they don't break when lightly folded. You want a bit of crunch left in the leaf.

Keep unfolding cabbage leaves and removing them when they get soft, all the way to the core. Set aside until cool enough to handle.

To make the filling, cook buckwheat following instructions on the package with a teaspoon of salt. Once cooked, drain and place in a mixing bowl.

Dice onion, wash and slice mushrooms. In a medium sauté pan, heat butter, add onion and mushrooms and a pinch of salt. Sauté until golden brown around the edges. Add to buckwheat. Season with pepper, thyme, salt, granulated onion, and garlic. Taste, add a bit more salt to taste.

Add a whole egg. Mix well.

Once cabbage has cooled off, with a sharp knife, remove / shave off veins of each leaf (see picture).

Continued on the next page.

When ready to bake, preheat oven to 350°F / 180°C. I'm using an oblong 12 x 8 inch / 30 x 23 centimeter baking dish, but a square 9 x 9 inch / 22 x 22 centimeter will work also.

To make rolls, place as much of the filling as you think you can fit onto a cabbage leaf (it will depend on the size; for a larger one it will be about ½ cup) and fold up from the stem end of the leaf up. Fold the sides in and keep rolling until you cover all of the filling. Place in the baking dish seam down.

Once your dish is filled with rolls, cover them with the remaining leaves too small to make rolls. You want the whole surface of the cabbage rolls covered. If you don't have enough leaves to cover all rolls, use tin foil when baking.

Bake for 45 minutes. While rolls are cooking, make sauce. I recommend tomato (recipe on pg. 118).

Buttered String Beans

— Fasolka szparagowa —

String beans covered in buttery bread crumbs is a delicious dish often served in spring time in Poland. We like it with a side of young potatoes and an egg over-easy, all garnished with fresh and fragrant dill.

Yields: *3–4 servings* **Prep time:** *5 minutes* **Cook time:** *15 minutes*

About 20 oz / 500 g of string green beans or yellow wax beans

¼ c of bread crumbs

3 tsp / 15 g of butter

Salt

Wash string beans and cut off ends. Boil until tender, for about 10–12 minutes, in salted water (I like mine with a little crunch). Drain, place in a serving bowl and cover to keep warm.

Place the bread crumbs in a small pan (no butter yet) and toast them until golden brown. Watch them closely and stir often; they will burn fast. When they reach the desired golden brown color, add butter and stir until melted. It should be bubbly and quite watery. If you feel the mixture is too dry, add an extra teaspoon of butter.

Pour mixture over hot string beans and serve.

Cauliflower or aspar-agus can also be served this way! Be creative!

Cabbage with Mushrooms

—Kapusta z grzybami—

"Kapusta z grzybami" is a vegetarian version of "bigos", which Poles often call "bigos jarski". It is prepared with both fresh cabbage and sauerkraut, dried wild mushrooms, fresh mushrooms, and spices. It's tangy and aromatic, and fills my kitchen with smells of the home I grew up in. This dish is often prepared for a vegetarian Christmas Eve dinner.

Yields: *5-6 servings* **Prep time:** *10 minutes* **Cook time:** *1.5 hours*

About 1 c / 20 g of dried mushrooms

½ head of a medium cabbage

3 bay leaves

6 whole peppercorns and allspice berries (each)

1 tsp salt

One 14 oz / 500 g can of sauerkraut

16–20 oz / 500–700 g of baby bellas / button mushrooms

3 tbsp of butter

1 large onion, chopped

2 tbsp of tomato paste

Place dried mushrooms in a small pot, add enough boiling water to cover, set aside until mushrooms rehydrate a bit (about 10–15 minutes).

In the meantime, shred cabbage and cut into smaller pieces. Place in a large pot with 1 ½ cups / 350 millilitres of water, bay leaves, peppercorns, allspice berries, and salt. Boil on medium heat until cabbage softens (only about 5 minutes). Add sauerkraut (I don't drain my sauerkraut, nor do I rinse it. If you like your kraut a bit milder, rinse and drain it before this step). Continue cooking on medium-low.

Clean and slice button mushrooms. Sauté in butter until golden brown around the edges, then add them to the cabbage mixture. Sauté chopped onion (add a bit more butter if needed), and also add to the pot.

After dried mushrooms rehydrate, boil for about 10 minutes on low (check if they're soft; if not, boil for a bit longer. Add more water if needed). When mushrooms are soft, dump the water from boiling them into the cabbage mixture. Chop wild mushrooms and also add to the cabbage.

Add tomato paste and continue cooking for a total cooking time of about 1 hour. Turn off and set aside to cool. Best if cooked again the next day. Refrigerate overnight. Next day, cook for another hour and a half or so, stirring occasionally.

Carrot Salad

– Surówka z marchwi –

Fresh and sweet salad;
a perfect addition to any main dish.

Yields: *4–5 servings*   **Prep time:** *10 minutes*

4–5 medium carrots
1 sweet apple
Juice of ½ a lemon
½ tsp sugar
Pinch of salt

Peel carrots and apple and grate on the largest side of a box grater. Mix to combine.

Add lemon juice, sugar, and salt.

Mix and cool in the fridge before serving.

My childhood favorite!

Celery Salad

— Surówka z selera —

*Raw salad made from celery root with sweet cream and lemon.
It is a great addition to any main dish.*

Yields: *5–6 servings*   **Prep time:** *10 minutes*

1 raw celery root (about 3 c grated)

1 tsp of sugar

Pinch of salt

Juice of ½ a lemon

1–1 ½ c / 235–350 ml of cream (sweet whipping cream or half and half; not sour cream)

Ground pepper to taste

Cut away the skin of the celery root and grate on the largest side of a box grater.

Place grated celery root in a mixing bowl, sprinkle with sugar, salt and pepper, lemon juice. Add cream and mix.

Refrigerate until serving.

Creamed Beets

— Buraczki zasmażane —

*This warm beet salad is such a perfect balance of sweet, tangy, and creamy.
It makes a great addition to a meat-and-potatoes kind of dinner.*

Yields: *3–4 servings*   **Prep time:** *10 minutes + 1 hour for roasting beets*

3 medium beets
2 tbsp / 30 g of butter
2 tbsp of all-purpose flour
½ tsp sugar
¼ c / 60 ml of sweet cream
3 tbsp of white vinegar
Pinch of salt

Preheat oven to 350°F / 180°C. Wash beets and roast in the oven (covered) until soft (about 1 hour).

Remove from the oven and cool.

*Peel and grate on the smallest side of a box grater (yep, the one that takes finger tips off - **careful!**)*

In a medium saucepan, heat butter on low, add flour to make roux. Whisk until combined and bubbly, about 30 seconds.

Add grated beets and the rest of the ingredients, heat through. Taste and add a bit more salt, if needed.

Cucumber Salad

— Mizeria —

*One of Poland's favorite summer salads,
made from crunchy cucumbers, sour cream, and aromatic dill.*

Yields: *2–3 servings*   **Prep time:** *15 minutes*

1 English cucumber (or 6–8 small pickling cucumbers)

¼ tsp salt

⅔ c / 150 ml sour cream

1 tbsp of fresh dill

Squeeze of a lemon

Pinch of pepper

Wash and peel the cucumber. Slice thin. Add salt and let sit for 10 minutes.

After 10 minutes, drain any water that may have accumulated.

Add sour cream and dill, a squeeze of lemon, and a pinch of pepper. Mix and chill until ready to serve.

Daikon Salad

— Surówka z rzodkwi —

Snowy-white and sharp-in-flavor daikon, combined with yogurt, lemon, and spices, makes a fun and unusual salad to accompany a bold main dish.

Yields: *4–5 servings*　**Prep time:** *10 minutes*

1 daikon
¼ c / 60 ml of plain yogurt
¼ c / 60 ml of heavy cream
Juice of ½–1 lemon
½ tsp sugar
¼ tsp salt

Wash and peel daikon. Grate on the largest side of a box grater.

Place in a bowl, add yogurt, heavy cream, lemon, sugar, and salt. Mix, and taste. If too dry, add another tablespoon of cream and yogurt. It should be pretty moist, but not soupy.

Chill until serving.

Fresh Cabbage Salad

— Surówka z kapusty —

*Crunchy salad made from fresh cabbage,
with carrots and sweet apple.*

Yields: *5–6 servings* **Prep time:** *15 minutes*

½ head of small cabbage (about 4 c shredded)

Pinch of salt

1 carrot

1 apple

¼ of a medium onion, minced

½ tsp of sugar

Juice of ½ a lemon

Shred your cabbage into thin pieces. Place in a mixing bowl, sprinkle with salt and mix with hands, squeezing the cabbage to soften it and to release the juices.

Grate carrot and apple on the largest side of a box grater and add to the mixing bowl with cabbage. Add onion. Sprinkle with sugar and add lemon juice.

Mix well and let sit for a couple of minutes to let the salt and sugar dissolve. Mix again and refrigerate until serving.

Fried Cabbage

— Kapusta zasmażana —

Creamy, sweet and sour cabbage, spiked with bits of smoky bacon and garnished with fresh dill is often prepared in early spring when new cabbage is in season.

Yields: *8–10 servings*   **Prep time:** *10 minutes*   **Cook time:** *20 minutes*

1 medium cabbage (about 2 lbs / 1 kg)

1 ½ c / 350 ml water

½ tsp salt

10 whole peppercorns and all-spice berries (each)

½ c / 120 ml white vinegar (4%)

4 thick slices of smoked bacon (about 6 oz / 170 g)

½ a medium onion, chopped

3 tbsp / 40 g of butter

3 tbsp of all-purpose flour

½ c fresh dill

Chop cabbage, as you would to make coleslaw. Place in a medium pot, add water, salt, peppercorns and allspice berries. Cook cabbage for only about 5 minutes. You want to preserve some crunch. Add vinegar, stir and set aside.

Chop bacon and sauté in a separate pan. When the edges start getting a little brown, add chopped onion. Sauté together for another few minutes, until nice and golden brown. Transfer into the cabbage mixture, reserving as much fat as possible.

To the now empty bacon pan, add butter and flour to make roux. Whisk while it heats for about 45–60 seconds. Transfer to cabbage mixture.

Turn cabbage to low heat and cook uncovered until some of the water evaporates and the dish thickens, for about 10–15 minutes.

Add chopped dill and taste. Add salt, if needed. Serve hot.

Enjoy as part of dinner, on a bed of potatoes or your favorite potato dumplings. You can also serve with sausage or a pork chop or as a side to your Thanksgiving dinner.

Anna's note:

TO STORE: *place sauerkraut into sanitized jars and keep in the fridge for up to 6 months.*

TO PASTEURIZE: *place sauerkraut in sanitized jars, making sure there is enough brine to cover (to make more brine, dissolve 1 tablespoon of salt in 1 quart of water and top up each jar). Place jars in a large pot, add water to just below the lid. Bring water to boil and simmer on low for 25 - 30 minutes. Remove and cool. Jars can now be stored unrefrigerated.*

Homemade Sauerkraut

—Kiszona kapusta—

Polish-style fermented cabbage is prepared in the fall. It will provide a supply of sauerkraut all the way through to the next pickling season.

Prep time: *30 minutes* **Fermenting time:** *10–12 days*

A glass, ceramic, or plastic pickling dish

Shredded cabbage

Shredded carrots (one carrot per 2 lbs / 1 kg of shredded cabbage)

1 tbsp / 20 g of rock or sea salt for every 2.2 lbs / 1 kg of shredded veggies (use non-iodized salt only!)

Sanitize the pickling dish with boiling water.

Thinly slice the cabbage or shred on a mandoline. Grate the carrots on the largest side of a box grater. At this point, I like to weigh my vegetables and measure out all of the salt I will need for the entirety of the dish.

Place shredded cabbage and carrots (about 1 kg / 2 lbs at a time) in a large mixing bowl / bucket and sprinkle with a bit of salt (1 tablespoon at a time). Mix and massage the cabbage until it produces some juice.

Place in a clean pickling dish and push down with force to make sure cabbage is covered with brine. Continue until you use up all of the shredded cabbage and carrots.

If you have a pressing stone, use it; if not, place a small plate on top of the cabbage mixture and top with a heavy sanitized dish or a jar full of water. Cover the top of the dish with a clean kitchen towel. Place on the kitchen counter for 10 days.

After 3 days, with the handle of a wooden spoon, poke holes in the cabbage to release gas. If there is excess water forming on top, remove it. There needs to be enough just to cover the cabbage. Reserve brine and use to replenish, if needed. Cabbage will be ready when it becomes translucent. It should be deliciously tangy and crunchy.

Leek Salad

— Surówka z pora —

Another creamy salad flavored with sweet carrot and apple.
Leeks are slightly spicy but cooled a bit by cold sour cream.

Yields: *4–5 servings*   **Prep time:** *15 minutes*

1 leek
1 carrot
1 apple
½ c / 120 ml of sour cream
A pinch of salt and pepper
Juice of ½ of a lemon

Cut off dry ends of the leek, if any, and thinly slice the rest of the vegetable at a 45° angle–it will look pretty.

Place sliced leek in a colander and rinse throughly to wash out any dirt or sand that may be remaining. Boil a small pot of water (about 6 cups / 1.5 liters) and pour over the leek. This will soften the vegetable and take away some of the sharpness. Let drain and cool.

In the meantime, wash carrot and apple and grate both on the largest side of a box grater. Place in a bowl and immediately stir in sour cream (we don't want the apple turning brown).

Once the leek has cooled off, add to the carrot / apple mixture along with a pinch of salt and pepper and lemon juice. Mix well and cool before serving.

Mushroom Cream Sauce

— Sos grzybowy —

Creamy sauce often prepared in late summer and early fall in Poland, when wild mushrooms are in season.

Yields: *5–6 servings*   **Prep time:** *15 minutes*   **Cook time:** *20 minutes*

14 oz / 400 g of fresh mushrooms (chanterelles*, oyster, portobello, shiitake or button mushrooms)

2 tbsp of butter

1 medium onion, diced

2 c / 500 ml of chicken or vegetable broth

½ tsp of pepper

1 c / 250 ml sweet cream

2 tbsp of all-purpose flour

Small bunch of parsley leaves, chopped

Wash mushrooms well (chanterelles tend to be quite sandy) and roughly chop into smaller pieces.

In a large saucepan, heat butter, add chopped onion and sauté until caramelized. Add mushrooms and sauté for about 15 minutes. Add broth and pepper, keep cooking.

In a jar or bowl, add flour to cream and mix well. Add mixture to sauce and bring sauce up to boil to thicken.

Lastly, add chopped parsley and stir to combine. Serve over favorite dumplings, cutlet, pasta, or grain.

Anna's note:

*I like using chanterelles when they are in season, but any fresh mushroom will do.

Onion Rolls

— Cebulaki; cebularze —

Soft yeast rolls topped with caramelized onions and baked til golden brown. These absolutely delicious savory buns can be served with soups or enjoyed just on their own.

Yields: *8 rolls* **Prep time:** *1–2 hours* **Cook time:** *30 minutes*

8 tbsp / 110 g of butter

1 c / 225 ml warm milk

2 ½ c / 450 g of all-purpose flour (+ ½ c for blooming yeast)

1 tbsp of dry yeast

1 tsp sugar

½ tsp salt

4 eggs yolks (+ 1 egg white)

1 tsp of oil

TOPPING:

2 ½ c of sliced onion

2 tbsp / 30 g of butter

¼ tsp of salt

¼ tsp of ground black pepper

1 ½ tbsp of poppyseeds

Melt butter, set aside to cool.

Place warm milk and ½ cup of flour in a mixing bowl, add yeast and sugar. Mix well and let yeast bloom until bubbles appear (about 10–15 minutes).

In a mixing bowl, place the rest of the flour, add bloomed yeast mixture and, with the hook attachment of a stand mixer, start mixing. Add butter, salt, and egg yolks and continue mixing until combined. Keep kneading for another 10 minutes. If not using a mixer, place your ingredients in a large bowl and work with your hands to form a dough ball. Transfer onto a floured surface and knead for 10 minutes, until dough is smooth.

Place dough in an oiled bowl, cover with a cloth and let rest and rise for 1–2 hours (or until the dough doubles in size).

Line a 9 x 11 inch / 23 x 28 centimeter baking pan with parchment paper.

Remove dough from bowl and place on a floured surface. Fold 3–4 times and create an even log. Cut log into 8 relatively even pieces. From each piece, form a ball and place on parchment paper. Cover with a cloth and let rest for 30 minutes.

In the meantime, cut the onion in half and into slices. In a medium sauté pan, heat butter, add onion, salt, pepper and sauté until translucent. Once cooked, turn off, add poppyseeds and stir to combine.

Preheat oven to 395°F / 200°C.

After rolls have been resting for about 30 minutes, flatten them lightly with your fingers. Whisk 1 egg white and brush over rolls, then cover evenly with sautéed onions.

Bake for 30–35 minutes, or until golden brown. Remove from oven and let cool slightly before moving onto a cooling rack.

Serve warm or cold.

⇨1 Before resting

⇨2 Before baking

2-Day Dill Pickles

— Ogórki matosolne —

*Pickles are fermented in salted brine for a couple of days only.
They are still fresh and crunchy.*

Prep time: *10 minutes*   **Fermenting time:** *2–3 days*

3.7 lbs / 1700 g pickling cucumbers

2–3 (about pencil-sized) sticks of fresh horseradish root, peeled

1 bunch of dill (best for pickling is dill with flowers and seeds, if you can find it)

8–10 garlic cloves

1–2 green onions or a sliver of leek - white and green parts

2–3 horseradish leaves, if you have

3–4 grape, cherry tree, currant, or oak leaves

2 qts / 2 l of water*

2 tbsp / 40 g of sea or rock salt (non-iodized)

ADDITIONALLY:

A 4-qt pickling crock or a glass jar

Wash cucumbers. Peel horseradish root and wash the rest of the ingredients.

Sanitize your crock / jar with boiling water and place all ingredients (minus the salt and water) in the crock. Be very diligent with sanitizing.

Bring water to boil and add salt, stir until dissolved. Pour hot water over cucumbers to fill the crock all the way. Cover with a small ceramic plate so everything is submerged.

Leave on the counter to pickle. Start tasting after 24 hours of pickling, then test them regularly to see the difference. They will change flavor daily and can be kept on the counter until all gone.

After a few days, they will change color from fresh green to a bit more subtle green. They are meant to be consumed after just 2–3 days of fermenting, but further fermentation is also fine.

If you see a white, cloudy residue on the bottom or on the cucumbers, don't be alarmed. It is lactic acid, a normal byproduct of fermentation. Just make sure all pickles are submerged in brine.

Anna's note:

General ratio for pickling cucumbers in brine is 1 to 1 (1 tablespoon of salt to 1 quart / 1 liter of water). You may adjust the recipe for larger containers using this simple rule.

Pickles in Brine

— Ogórki kiszone —

Pickles are placed in jars and fermented in salted brine. They are a bit softer than a vinegar-based pickle and have the distinct flavor of sour pickle. We use them to prepare pickle soup or enjoy on sandwiches, in salads, or just on their own.

Prep time: *10 minutes*   **Fermenting time:** *4–7 days*

Pickling cucumbers

SPICES PER QUART / LITER JAR:

One 3 inch / 5 cm stick of horseradish root, peeled

1 (or more) twigs of fresh dill

3 garlic cloves

Leaves of horseradish plant, oak, cherry tree, grape leaves, or currant leaves

1 bay leaf

BRINE RATIO:

1 qt / 1 l of water

1 tbsp / 20 g of sea or rock salt

ADDITIONALLY:

Pickling jars and lids

Large pot for disinfecting and pickling jars

Sanitize jars and lids in boiling water. Wash cucumbers and set aside. Peel horseradish root and cut into long strips (about ½ x 5 inch / 1 x 8 centimeter). Wash dill and peel garlic.

In a pot, boil water, and when hot, add salt–**see brine ratio***–adjust to desired amount of jars.

Place a layer of dill on the bottom of each jar. Arrange the cucumbers to fit as many as you can to fill the jar. Place garlic, horseradish and leaves in between the cucumbers. Add more dill on top.

Pour hot salt brine to cover the contents. Place cover on top of the jar, close tightly and leave at room temperature.

Pickles are ready when brine turns murky and cloudy (4–7 days). Lids will bulge out as the brine sours, this is normal.

Store unrefrigerated.

Best for pickle soup!

Anna's note:

*General brine ratio for pickling cucumbers in brine is 1 to 1 (1 tablespoon of salt to 1 quart / 1 liter of water). You may adjust the recipe to yield more servings using this simple rule.

Vinegar Dill Pickles

— Ogórki konserwowe —

"Ogórki konserwowe" are pickles prepared in vinegar-based brine. They are mainly enjoyed on sandwiches and in salads.

Prep time: *20 minutes*   **Pickling time:** *2–3 days*

4 lbs / 2 kg of pickling cucumbers

BRINE:

5 c / 1.2 l of water

2 c / 500 ml of vinegar (4 %)

½ c / 100 g of granulated sugar

1 tbsp of salt

SPICES:

1 bunch of dill - 3 twigs per jar (or more)

2–3 garlic cloves per jar

1 medium horseradish root, cut into about ½ x 4 inch / 1 x 10 cm sticks (3 sticks per jar)

1 bay leaf per jar

10 whole peppercorns per jar

2 whole allspice berries per jar

1 tsp of mustard seed per jar

OPTIONAL:

Spicy peppers (as many as you would like to make spicy pickles)

ADDITIONALLY:

Five 1 qt / 1 l jars and lids

Large pot for disinfecting and pickling jars

Sanitize jars and lids in boiling water.

In a medium pot, combine brine ingredients and heat through.

Wash cucumbers and dill. Peel garlic and horseradish root. Cut horseradish into sticks. Place cucumbers and all spices in each jar.

Pour brine into each jar and place covers on tightly. Place jars back into hot water up to just below the lid. Bring to boil. Boil on low for 3 minutes from the time the water starts bubbling. Take jars out and cool.

Pickles will be ready in 2–3 days and can be stored unrefrigerated.

Potato Cake

— Babka ziemniaczana —

"Babka ziemniaczana" is also known as "kartoflak" and is a savory cake served as a side dish. I like it as a side to a wild mushroom sauce or next to a grilled sausage.

Yields: *6–8 servings* **Prep time:** *30 minutes* **Cook time:** *70–90 minutes*

2.5 lbs / 1 kg of raw potatoes

2 medium onions, chopped

6 oz / 200 g of lean, smoked bacon

1–2 tsp of fresh herbs (thyme, rosemary, or parsley)

2 eggs

½ tsp salt

¼ tsp ground pepper

⅓ c / 40 g of all-purpose flour

Peel and dice potatoes. Keep submerged in cold water until ready to blend.

Dice onion and bacon. Sauté bacon on medium heat for about 5 minutes, until some of the fat melts. Add onion and sauté together until golden brown. Set aside. Chop the herbs.

Preheat oven to 350°F / 180°C.

Grease a 9 x 5 inch / 23 x 13 centimeter loaf pan with butter or line with parchment paper.

Place potatoes, eggs, salt and pepper in a blender and blend until smooth (you can also use a hand grater to grate potatoes; use the smallest side of a box grater; add eggs and spices to mixture once grated).

When blended, place in a large mixing bowl, add herbs, flour, bacon, and onions, and hand mix until combined. Pour mixture into the loaf pan.

Bake for about 90 minutes, until the outside is golden brown and the middle is dry and set.

Serve sliced after baking or reheat by placing slices in butter and sautéing each side until golden brown.

Try reheating slices in butter and serving with morning eggs!

Potato Salad

— Sałatka ziemniaczana —

*Classic salad full of herbs and aromatics,
makes a great all-year-round addition to your party table.*

Yields: *5–6 servings*   **Prep time:** *30–40 minutes*

5–6 medium waxy potatoes (I like red)

4 hard-boiled eggs

4 pickles

½ a white onion or 3 whole green onions

½ c / 120 ml of mayonnaise

3 tbsp of fresh dill (or parsley or both), chopped

2 garlic cloves, minced

¼ tsp of salt

¼ tsp of freshly ground pepper

Wash potatoes and boil, skin on, in salted water. Boil eggs. Cool both.

Dice potatoes (about ½ inch / 2 centimeter cubes), peeling excess skin off and leaving some of the skin on. Peel and dice eggs, dice pickles and mince the onion (or green onions). Place all in a large mixing bowl.

Add remaining ingredients. Mix well. Taste. Add more salt, if needed.

Cool and mix again before serving.

Prepared Horseradish & Horseradish with Beets

– Chrzan i ćwikła z chrzanem –

This condiment is famous for it's sharpness and spicy flavor. We serve it with cold cuts and sausages and it is always present on our Easter table.

Yields: *2 cups*   **Prep time:** *10 minutes + 1 hour for cooking beets*

– Prepared Horseradish –

1 horseradish root (10 inch / 25 cm)

½ tbsp of sugar

Juice of 1 lemon

16 oz / 475 ml of sweet cream

Pinch of salt

To make creamy horseradish sauce, peel the horseradish root, slice and place in a blender with the rest of the ingredients. Blend until smooth. Transfer into jars and store in the fridge.

– Horseradish with Beets –

1 large beetroot, cooked

1 horseradish root (10 inch / 25 cm)

Juice of 1 lemon

½ c / 120 ml of water

½ tbsp of sugar

Pinch of salt

To make horseradish with beets, boil an unpeeled beet until cooked (about 45 minutes); cool, peel and dice. Peel horseradish root and roughly chop.

Place all ingredients in a blender and blend for 30 seconds, until smooth. Transfer into jars and store in the fridge.

Red Cabbage Salad

– Surówka z czerwonej kapusty –

Simple, fresh, and crunchy salad with a lemon-based dressing, often served as a side to meaty sauces.

Yields: *3–4 servings* **Prep time:** *15 minutes*

½ head of red cabbage (about 5 c shredded)

½ tsp salt

1 apple

¼ of a small onion (about 3 tbsp)

Juice of ½ lemon

½ tsp sugar

1 tbsp of vegetable oil

Take your time and thinly shred the cabbage. Sprinkle with salt and massage for a couple of minutes to release juices.

Grate the apple and mince the onion. Add to cabbage, along with lemon juice, sugar, and oil. Mix until combined.

Chill until serving. Serve as a dinner veggie side.

Perfect side for grilled meats!

Red Cabbage with Apples

—Modra kapusta z jabłkami—

This traditional dish of creamy red cabbage is often served with duck or goose. It succesfully breaks up the rich flavor of the meat and joins the two in a perfect marriage of savory and sweet, crunchy and creamy.

Yields: *8–10 servings*   **Prep time:** *10 minutes*   **Cook time:** *15 minutes*

1 head of red cabbage (about 2 lbs / 1 kg)

1 ½ c / 350 ml of water

2 bay leaves

4 whole peppercorns and allspice berries (each)

1 tsp salt

1 apple

4 tbsp / 55 g of butter

3 tbsp of all-purpose flour

¼ c / 60 ml of white vinegar (4%)

½ tsp of sugar

Cut cabbage into quarters and shred by hand or using a mandoline. Place in a medium pot with water, add bay leaves, peppercorns, allspice berries, and salt and heat through only until it softens a bit (about 5–7 minutes).

Wash, peel and core the apple and grate it on the largest side of a box grater.

In a separate small saucepan, melt butter on low-medium heat. Add flour, whisk well and brown for about 30 seconds. Add to cabbage. Also add vinegar, sugar, and apple, and stir.

Cook over medium heat until water evaporates, stirring occasionally (about 15 minutes). Cabbage should become softer, but keep a little bit of the crunch.

Sauerkraut & Mushroom Pies

— Paszteciki z kapustą i grzybami —

Delicious savory pies can be prepared with a variety of fillings:
meat, mushroom, or sauerkraut and mushroom.
They are a great snack or a party starter.

Yields: *12 pies* **Prep time:** *20 minutes* **Cook time:** *40–45 minutes*

DOUGH:

3 ¼ c / 400 g of all-purpose flour

1 ¼ c / 300 ml warm water

1 tsp of salt

1 ½ tsp of instant yeast

FILLING:

6 oz / 170 g of mushrooms (baby bella, crimini or portobello mushrooms)

1 onion, chopped

2 tbsp of butter or oil

Pinch of salt

3 bay leaves

6 whole peppercorns and all-spice berries (each)

¼ tsp of ground pepper

One 14 oz / 400 g can of sauerkraut

ADDITIONALLY:

1 egg

Serve with beetroot broth, recipe on page 23.

Combine ingredients to form dough. Knead until smooth (3–5 minutes). Set aside, covered, in a warm spot. Rest until filling is ready.

Chop clean mushrooms and sauté in butter with onions and a pinch of salt until they're brown around the edges. Add bay leaves, peppercorns, allspice berries, and ground pepper.

Drain sauerkraut and roughly chop. Add to mushroom / onion mixture and sauté until all liquid evaporates (about 10 minutes)–make sure the mixture is completely dry. Set aside to cool.

Preheat oven to 350°F / 180°C.

Divide dough in half and roll out to form a rectangle. Place half of sauerkraut and mushroom filling along the middle of the rolled out dough. Brush edges of the dough (all around) with beaten egg. Fold top half of the rectangle onto filling, and then the bottom onto the dough (see photos). Flip stuffed roll upside down, onto the seam. Cut into smaller sections but don't spread out.

Transfer onto a baking sheet lined with parchment paper. Even though each roll is cut, keep cut pieces close together (along the cuts) so the filling doesn't spill out and dry out.

Bake for about 15–20 minutes, or until the top is golden brown.

Anna's note:

To make meat filling, use the recipe for making meat pierogi.

221

Sauerkraut Salad

– Surówka z kiszonej kapusty –

*Crunchy, sweet and sour salad, best if made from homemade sauerkraut.
We often enjoy it as a side dish to fried fish.*

Yields: *5–6 servings*   **Prep time:** *10 minutes*

1 carrot

1 apple

One 8 oz / 225 g can of sauerkraut, drained

¼ of a medium onion, minced

½ tsp of sugar

1 tbsp of vegetable oil

Pinch of salt

Peel carrot and apple, grate on the largest side of a box vegetable grater and add to the mixing bowl with sauerkraut. Add onion. Sprinkle with sugar and add oil.

Mix well and let sit for a couple of minutes to let the sugar dissolve. Mix again and taste. Add salt if needed.

Tomato & Onion Salad

— Pomidory z cebulą —

Very popular salad while tomatoes are in season. Ripe and juicy tomatoes combined with crunchy and spicy onion are so refreshing on a hot summer day.

Yields: *3–4 servings*   **Prep time:** *10 minutes*

5–6 medium, ripe tomatoes

½ a medium onion

¼ c / 60 ml of sour cream (plain yogurt also works well)

Pinch of salt and pepper

Wash and dry tomatoes. Cut into good-sized chunks. Thinly slice the onion. Add sour cream, salt, and pepper. Mix.

If too dry, add a bit more sour cream, but let sit for a few minutes; it will become more watery.

Chill before serving.

Vegetable Salad

— Sałatka jarzynowa —

Traditional Polish salad served on all holidays and special occasions.
Even though it takes a bit of time to make, everyone is always looking forward to
it. It is the ultimate comfort food.

Yields: *8–10 servings* **Prep time:** *30–40 minutes*

3 medium, waxy potatoes
3 carrots
1 parsley root (or parsnip)
3 eggs
1 stick of celery
4–5 of your favorite pickles
½ a small onion
1 apple
3–4 sticks of green onion
¾ c of raw, frozen peas
Handful of parsley
½ c of mayonaise
Salt and pepper

Boil potatoes, carrots and parsley / parsnip in salted water until tender. Hard boil eggs. Let cool.

Dice up celery, pickles, onion, apple, and the green onions into small, even pieces. Once potatoes, carrots, and eggs cool down, also dice into small pieces.

In a large mixing bowl, combine all ingredients, add peas and parsley. Sprinkle with salt and pepper, add mayo and gently mix until combined. Taste.

If you feel it's too dry, add another tablespoon of mayo. Add more salt and pepper, if needed.

Desserts

Desery

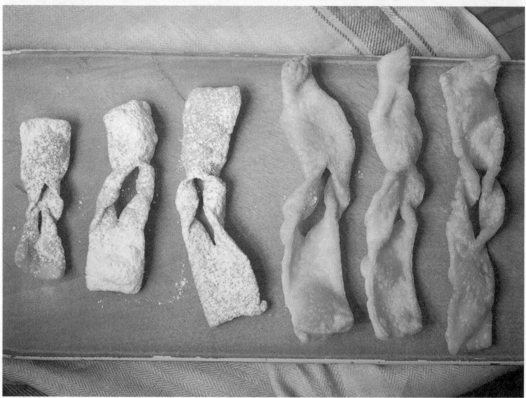

Angel Wings

— Faworki / Chrust —

*Thin fried cookies
sprinkled with powdered sugar.*

Prep time: *20 minutes*   **Cook time:** *45–60 minutes*

4 ½ c / 585 g of bread flour
+ ½ c for dusting

Pinch of salt

7 eggs

3 tbsp of sour cream

1 ½ tbsp of butter, melted and cooled

2 tbsp of 75 % / 151 proof alcohol

Oil for frying

Powdered sugar

In a mixing bowl, place flour and salt. In a separate bowl, mix eggs with sour cream. Add to flour. Start mixing to combine. Add butter and alcohol and continue to mix until dough forms.

Sprinkle some flour onto a clean surface and transfer dough onto it. Continue kneading and punching the dough for no less than 10 minutes.

*Cut a small section of the dough and roll out into a **thin** sheet. With a pizza cutter, cut into 1 inch / 3 centimeter strips, and then each strip into smaller pieces— see photo.*

Cut a small slit in the middle of each piece. Bring the bottom of the piece up toward the slit and pull it through to create the curly sides.

In a deep frying pan / cast iron skillet heat oil (enough oil to be about 2 inches in depth) and fry dough strips until golden brown. You will have to flip them. Remove and place on a sheet covered with paper towels. Once cool, sprinkle with powdered sugar.

Apple Cake

— Jabłecznik —

Traditional shortbread-crust cake with apple filling, one of the most favorite of my cakes. Grandma made this almost weekly, to enjoy with Sunday dinner.

Yields: *10–12 servings*   **Prep time:** *1 hour*   **Cook time:** *45–50 minutes*

CRUST:

1 whole egg

1 yolk (reserve the egg white)

1 c / 120 g of powdered sugar

2 ½ c / 315 g of all-purpose flour

1 tsp of baking powder

Zest of ½ lemon

7 oz / 200 g of cold butter

FILLING:

10 tart apples

¼ c / 50 g of granulated sugar

Zest and juice of ½ lemon

¼ tsp of cinnamon

To prepare the crust: whip the egg and an egg yolk with sugar. Add flour, baking powder, and lemon zest. Cut cold butter into small cubes and also add to the mixture. Mix and knead until just combined with the help of a utensil. Finished dough should have lumps of butter in it. Butter will make the crust flaky.

Wrap in plastic wrap and refrigerate for 1 hour.

To make the filling: peel and core apples. Grate on the largest side of a box vegetable grater and place in a deep frying pan. Add sugar, zest, and lemon juice and cook on medium until all juice evaporates (about 30 minutes). Set aside to cool.

When ready to bake, preheat the oven to 400° F / 200° C.

Grease the bottom and sides of a 9 x 9 inch / 23 x 23 centimeter baking dish with butter (or line with parchement paper).

Cut the dough in half, place between two pieces of parchment paper and roll out to fit your baking dish. Make sure there is enough dough to cover the sides as well. Distribute evenly on the bottom and all the way up the sides. Scoop the cool filling onto the bottom of the crust. Roll out the remaining half of the dough and place on top of the filling.

Whisk the egg white and a teaspoon of water with a fork, and brush onto the top of the crust.

Bake for 45–50 minutes or until crust is golden brown.

Bundt Cake

— Babka piaskowa —

*Traditional, simple cake baked in a bundt pan,
prepared and served at Easter.*

Yields: *6–8 servings*   **Prep time:** *10 minutes*   **Cook time:** *20–30 minutes*

5 eggs - separated

1 c / 200 g of granulated sugar

9 oz / 255 g of melted butter

¾ c / 95 g of all-purpose flour

¾ c / 90 g of potato flour (or corn starch)

2 tsp of baking powder

½ tsp vanilla

Zest of ½ a lemon

2 pinches of salt

1 tbsp of butter for greasing the pan

1 tbsp of bread crumbs for the pan

Preheat oven to 350°F / 180° C. Separate yolks from whites. Add sugar to yolks and beat until fluffy. Slowly add melted butter (not hot) and beat until combined.

Add flours, baking powder, a pinch of salt, vanilla, and lemon zest. Mix for a couple of minutes.

In a separate bowl, beat the egg whites with another pinch of salt until stiff, about 3 minutes. Add to cake mixture and gently fold until combined.

Grease bundt cake pan with butter and sprinkle bread crumbs to prevent cake from sticking. Transfer cake batter into pan and bake for 40–50 minutes.

Take out and cool. Serve topped with powdered sugar, chocolate ganache, or sugar glaze.

Recipe for a perfect chocolate ganache on page 237.

Cheesecake

Sernik

Traditional Polish cheesecake, best if made with real, homemade farmer's cheese, topped with chocolate ganache.

Yields: *8–10 servings*   **Prep time:** *20 minutes*   **Cook time:** *1 hour + cooling*

– Cake –

2.2 lbs / 1 kg of full-fat farmer's cheese

⅔ c / 5 fl oz / 150 ml whipping cream (30% fat)

7 oz / 200 g room-temperature butter

1 c / 200 g powdered sugar

6 large eggs - separated

1 tsp vanilla extract

¼ c / 50 g potato (or corn) starch

Zest of 1 medium orange

Pinch of salt

GANACHE:

½ c / 4 fl oz / 120 ml of whipping cream (30% fat)

3.5 oz / 100 g of dark chocolate

Pinch of cinnamon (optional)

DECORATIONS:

1 orange

3 sticks of cinnamon

A few star anise

Turn oven on to 340°F / 170°C. Prepare 11 inch / 28 centimeter round springform pan by lining the bottom with parchment paper; also cut a long strip of paper to line the sides.

Place farmer's cheese in a food processor and blend with whipping cream until smooth (about 5 minutes). Set aside.

In the large bowl of a stand mixer, place butter and powdered sugar. Whisk until fluffy and light in color (about 5 minutes). Separate yolks from egg whites. When eggs have been separated and butter / sugar mixture is ready, add egg yolks one by one and keep whisking. Slow down the speed of the whisk and start adding the cheese mixture. Add a few spoonfuls at a time, whisking continuously. Finally, add vanilla extract, potato (corn) starch, and orange zest. Whisk on low until combined.

In a separate bowl, whisk egg whites with a pinch of salt until stiff peaks form. Add egg whites to cheese mixture in portions and fold gently until combined.

Pour batter into springform pan and bake for 1 hour. When done baking, turn oven off and let cheesecake cool in the oven with the oven door cracked for at least 30 minutes. After that, take it out and cool completely before placing in the fridge. Cool in the fridge for at least 3-4 hours before making ganache.

*When ready to decorate, take cheesecake out of springform pan; with the help of a large plate or a cutting board, flip cheesecake to **remove paper from bottom** and sides, then transfer cheesecake onto a platter.*

— Ganache & Decorations —

To prepare ganache, heat cream in a small pot; do not boil. Break up the chocolate and place in a bowl. When cream is hot, pour it over chocolate and let sit for 2–3 minutes until chocolate melts. You can add a pinch of cinnamon to it if you'd like. After chocolate has melted completely, mix until smooth.

Pour chocolate ganache over the top of the cake and let cool for about 15 minutes before decorating and / or serving. Decorate with slices of orange, cinnamon sticks and star anise.

Chocolate "Mazurek"

— Mazurek z czekoladą —

Buttercrust bottom finished with a favorite topping. This traditional cake is only prepared once every year, when Poland is celebrating Easter.

Yields: *8–10 servings* **Prep time:** *3 hours* **Cook time:** *1 hour*

CRUST:

2 ½ c / 310 g of all-purpose flour

½ c of powdered sugar

1 tsp of baking powder

1 egg

2 yolks

7 oz / 200 g of cold butter

Zest of ½ a lemon

TOPPING:

One 14 oz / 400 g can of sweet-ened condensed milk

1 bar of 70% (or more) cacao chocolate (or about 3 oz / 85 g of chocolate chips)

1 tsp of butter

About ½ c of sliced almonds or hazelnuts

Take label off condensed milk can, place in a pot, fill with enough cold water to cover the can and boil on very low (just enough for bubbles to roll) for 3 hours. Remove and set aside to cool.

In the meantime, make the crust: combine all dry in-gredients, add egg (and yolks), cold butter, and lemon zest. Cut through with a knife and knead to form dough. Don't overwork it. Finished dough should have lumps of butter in it. It will just make the dough flaky.

Preheat oven to 350° F / 180° C.

Roll out by placing in between two pieces of parch-ment paper. Line a baking dish (just the bottom) with parchment paper, transfer rolled out dough and form into the desired shape. Press edges with a fork to create a decorative edge.

Bake for 30–35 minutes, until golden brown. Take out and cool. Careful when handling the crust: it's very frag-ile.

Once condensed milk in can cools, top crust with a hefty layer of condensed milk spread (open can when still a bit warm and contents are easily removed).

Place chocolate in a ceramic bowl and heat in the microwave in 15 second increments until melted. Add butter and mix. A spoonful of chocolate at a time, make swirls on top of the milk spread. Top with almonds. Let rest for a day or so before serving.

To serve, cut into bite-sized pieces.

Christmas Fruit Cake

— Keks świąteczny —

Soft and sweet cake spiked with nuts and dried fruit served during Polish Christmas. This cake will not disappoint with flavor and texture, and it is like no other fruit cake out there.

Yields: *8–10 servings*   **Prep time:** *10 minutes*   **Cook time:** *1 hour*

1 lb / 500 g of mixed, dried fruit and nuts—raisins, mangos, prunes, walnuts, almonds

8 oz / 225 g of butter at room temperature

1 c / 120 g of powdered sugar

5 eggs—whites and yolks separated

1 tsp of vanilla extract

2 c / 250 g of all-purpose flour

1 tbsp of baking powder

Pinch of salt

Preheat oven to 350°F / 180°C.

Crush and slice dried fruit and nuts.

Cream butter with sugar until well combined and fluffy. Add egg yolks one by one and keep mixing. Add vanilla extract and gradually add flour mixed with baking powder. Finally, add fruit / nut mixture.

In a separate bowl, whisk egg whites with salt on high speed until stiff foam forms. Gently fold into fruitcake batter until well combined.

Transfer batter into a loaf pan lined with parchment paper and bake at 350°F / 180°C for 20 minutes. Turn heat down to 325°F / 160°C and bake for another 30–40 minutes, until a toothpick inserted into cake comes out clean and top of the cake is golden brown. If top is browning too fast, cover with aluminum foil.

With the help of a small strainer, sprinkle with powdered sugar before serving.

Donuts

– Pączki –

Classic Polish yeast donuts;
can be filled with jelly or custard.

Yields: *50 small donuts* **Prep time:** *1.5 hours* **Cook time:** *1 hour*

– Pączki –

STARTER:

3.5 oz / 90 g of fresh yeast (or 4.5 tbsp of active dry yeast)

1 tbsp of sugar

1 ½ c / 200 g of bread flour

1 c / 300 ml of warm (not hot) milk

DOUGH:

6 egg yolks + 1 whole egg

½ c / 100 g of sugar

6 c / 800 g of bread flour

Additional ¾ c / 185 ml of warm (not hot) milk

Zest and juice of 1 lemon

3.5 tbsp / 50 ml of 75 % / 151 proof alcohol

Pinch of salt

1 tsp of vanilla extract

3.5 oz / 100 g of melted and cooled butter

2 lbs / 1 kg of lard (for frying)

Make starter by placing all ingredients in a bowl and mixing well to combine. Place bowl in a warm spot covered with a kitchen towel and let rise for 1 hour.

When the hour is almost up, make dough by whisking egg yolks, egg, and sugar in mixer bowl with a whisk attachment until white and fluffy (about 3–4 minutes).

Change whisk to a mixing paddle, add yeast starter and start mixing. Gradually start adding flour, alternating with milk. Also add lemon zest and juice, alcohol, salt, and vanilla extract. When it becomes too thick to mix with the mixing paddle, start kneading by hand. Knead until dough is smooth and it doesn't stick to your hands anymore (no less than 10 minutes).

Finally, slowly add melted butter and keep kneading until incorporated.

Place dough in a large bowl, cover with a kitchen towel and let rise for 1 hour or until it doubles in size.

After 1 hour, divide dough in half and roll out to about ½ inch / 2 centimeter thickness. With a glass or a metal can, cut out circles and place on a cookie sheet. Do this with all of your dough. Cover dough circles with a towel and let rise for 1 hour.

About 15 minutes before the hour is up, start heating the lard. Place it in a rather narrow pot (we'll be frying only 2–3 at a time, and we need some depth in the oil) and heat on medium til grease reaches 350°F / 180°C or slightly below (or until a piece of dough placed in grease starts bubbling immediately).

Be very careful with placing donuts into hot grease. I use a wire spoon to place 2 or 3 donuts at a time. Fry donuts until they are golden brown (about 2–3 minutes per side) and flip. Don't rush this process: we want to made sure dough cooks on the inside as well. If dough burns right away, turn heat down. Once golden brown, remove onto a paper-towel-lined sheet.

– Filling & Glaze –

FILLING:

1 jar of favorite jam

Powdered sugar (for garnish)

Or to make **GLAZE:**

2 c / 250 g of powdered sugar

Juice of 1 lemon

2–3 tbsp of water

Candied lemon peel (if you like)

If you'd like to fill them with jelly, let them cool first. Fill a pastry bag (with a long nozzle) with jelly. Insert nozzle into donut and push on bag to fill them with about 1 teaspoon of jelly.

I like mine with powdered sugar only, but if you'd like to glaze yours, place powdered sugar in a bowl, add lemon juice, then add water 1 tablespoon at a time until it reaches the desired consistency. Pour over donuts and garnish with lemon peel.

Gingerbread

— Piernik —

*Soft gingerbread with a layer of fruit jelly,
covered in chocolate ganache.*

Yields: *8–10 servings*   **Prep time:** *10 minutes*   **Cook time:** *60 minutes*

2 tbsp of honey

½ tsp of ground ginger

2 tsp of cinnamon

½ tsp of ground nutmeg

½ tsp of ground cloves

½ tsp of ground allspice

⅛ tsp of ground cardamom

2 tbsp of plum / strawberry / currant (or other favorite fruit) jam

Zest of ½ an orange

5 oz / 140 g of butter

1 c / 200 g of granulated sugar

2 eggs

1 c / 235 ml of milk

2 c / 250 g of all-purpose flour

2 tsp of baking powder

1 tsp of baking soda

A pinch of salt

ADDITIONALLY:

A few tablespoons of plum / strawberry / currant (or other favorite fruit) butter / jam

GLAZE:

½ c / 120 ml of whipping cream

3.5 oz / 100 g of dark chocolate

In a small saucepan, place honey, spices, jam, and orange zest and heat through. Set aside to cool.

Preheat oven to 350°F / 180°C. Line a bread loaf pan with parchment paper.

In a large mixing bowl, beat butter and sugar. Add eggs one at a time and then cooled honey mixture and milk. Stir well.

Mix flour with baking powder, baking soda, and salt. Add flour to sugar / butter mixture gradually and let combine well.

Transfer mixture into loaf pan and bake for 50–60 minutes, or until inserted toothpick comes out clean.

Cool bread completely before slicing in half horizontally from end to end. Spread jam onto the cut bottom part and return the top back onto it.

To make the glaze, heat cream in a small saucepan. Remove from heat and add broken up chocolate. Mix until melted and smooth. Cool glaze slightly before pouring over ginger bread.

No-bake Cheesecake

—Sernik na zimno —

Creamy no-bake cheesecake with fresh fruit and jello topping. This was my favorite birthday cake when I was little and I love to make it for my daughter. She is now also hooked.

Yields: *8–10 servings*   **Prep time:** *15 minutes + cooling*

35 oz / 1 kg of farmer's or plain cream cheese

2 envelopes (0.25 oz each) of un-flavored gelatin + 1 c of hot water

1 box (3 oz) of lemon jello + 1 c of hot water

¼ c / 30 g of powdered sugar

Vanilla wafers (round vanilla cookies)

TOPPING:

Fresh strawberries, raspberries, or other summer fruit

2 boxes (3 oz each) of strawberry jello

ADDITIONALLY:

9 inch / 23 cm or bigger round springform pan

*Leave cheese out to come to room temperature. In the meantime, dissolve 2 envelopes of gelatin in 1 cup hot water, and lemon jello in 1 cup of hot water (that's **half the water the recipe on the box calls for**). Set aside to cool.*

When cheese is ready, place in food processor and process for about 2 minutes. Add both gelatin and jello a little bit at a time. Keep processing until all lumps dissolve (about 2 minutes). Add sugar and process some more until combined.

Separate the walls of the spring form from the bottom. Line just the bottom with parchment paper, and secure the paper with the spring form walls. Cover the bottom with vanilla wafers. Pour cream cheese mixture into the pan. Refrigerate until set, at least 2 hours.

*Prepare strawberry jello with **half the water the recipe on the box calls for**—1 cup of water for each box. This means you will end up with 2 cups of jello as we're using two boxes. Let cool a bit.*

Wash and dry fresh berries and cut into smaller pieces, if needed. Arrange on top of set cheese mixture. Pour cooled jello over strawberries and refrigerate until cake sets (preferably overnight). Serve cold.

Poppyseed Roll

—Makowiec —

Traditional poppyseed-filled yeast dough roll, topped with powdered sugar glaze, accompanies us during every important event. It is a must have during Christmas holidays.

Yields: *2 rolls*   **Prep time:** *1 hour*   **Cook time:** *50–60 minutes*

FILLING:

¾ c / 100 g of raisins

About 17 oz / 500 g of raw black or blue poppyseeds

3 c / 750 ml of boiling water

4 oz / 110 g of butter

1 c / 200 g of granulated sugar

4 tbsp of honey

1 c / 100 g of walnuts

DOUGH:

¾ c / 150 ml of warm milk

1 ½ tbsp of active dry yeast

½ c / 100 g of granulated sugar

3 ½ c / 540 g of all-purpose flour

1 egg plus 2 yolks (large eggs) - reserve whites

2 oz / 55 g of butter

Pinch of salt

FOR GLAZE:

5 tbsp / 55 g of powdered sugar

2 tbsp of lemon juice

1 tbsp of hot water

3–5 tbsp of orange peel or sliced almonds

Place raisins in hot water (or rum, whiskey, or brandy) and set aside to soak.

Warm milk slightly, add yeast and sugar and set aside in a warm spot for 10 minutes. Melt butter (for dough) and set aside to cool slightly.

To make dough, place flour in a mixing bowl. Whisk egg and yolks and add to flour. Add milk / sugar / yeast mixture and start combining. Add melted butter and work to combine all ingredients. Add a few tablespoons of milk if dough is too dry. Dough should have consistency of playdough - not sticky but pliable. Once a dough ball is formed, cover and set aside in a warm place for at least 1 hour, until it doubles in size.

*To make filling, place poppyseeds in a pot, add boiling water and soak for 10 minutes, then boil for 20–25 minutes. Add a bit more water if they get dry, enough to cover. Drain well. Once they cool slightly you will have to put them through a meat grinder with the fine grinding plate - **TWICE**.*

In a large skillet or a pot, heat butter, add ground up poppyseeds, sugar, honey, drained raisins and mix well. Heat through and mix until sugar is dissolved. Add crushed walnuts and mix. Set aside to cool.

Whisk egg whites with a pinch of salt until stiff. Add to poppyseed mixture and fold in gently.

Continued on the next page.

pinch!   roll   pinch!

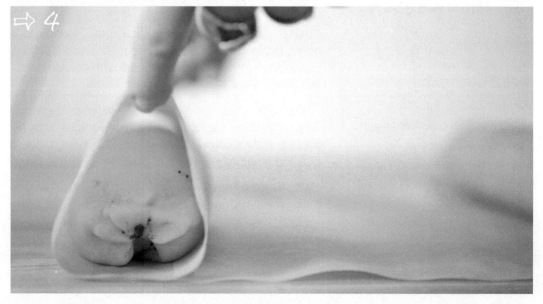

Once the dough rises, divide in half. Roll out each half into a rectangular shape (12 x 9 inch / 30 x 25 centimeter). Place rolled out dough onto parchment paper large enough to go around your roll twice. Place half of the filling on the first rectangle leaving a bit of space on each side (see photos). Roll starting from the wider edge, pinching the ends together as you go along. Wet the edge with water or egg white for a better seal.

Once rolled, make sure to leave on parchment paper with the long seam down. Roll parchment paper around the poppyseed roll twice, leaving space for the roll to "grow" (about ¾ inch / 2 centimeters). Make sure the end of the paper is under the roll. Set aside in a warm place to rise for about 30–45 minutes.

Do the same with the second roll.

When ready to bake, heat oven to 350°F / 180°C. Place rolls wrapped in paper in hot oven and bake for 40–50 minutes. Remove and cool.

To make glaze, mix powdered sugar with lemon juice. Add hot water one teaspoon at a time and whisk to combine. It should make a thick paste. If it comes out too watery, add more powdered sugar. Spoon onto each roll. Sprinkle with orange peel or almond shavings. Let set.

Raspberry Crumble Cake

– Ciasto z malinami i kruszonką –

Soft cake with tangy fruit and sweet crumble;
best made when fruit is in season.

Yields: *9 x 9 inch / 23 x 23 centimeter pan*　**Prep time:** *10 minutes*　**Cook time:** *50–55 minutes*

8 oz / 225 g of butter at room temperature

½ c / 100 g of granulated sugar

4 whole eggs

1 ½ c / 190 g of all-purpose flour

⅓ c / 40 g of potato flour (or corn starch)

2 tsp of baking powder

Pinch of salt

12 oz / 350 g of fresh raspberries

CRUMBLE TOPPING:

2 oz / 55 g of cold butter

½ c / 60 g of all-purpose flour

⅓ c / 40 g of powdered sugar

Preheat oven to 350°F / 180°C. Beat butter on high until fluffy (2–3 minutes), add sugar and beat for an additional 3 minutes. Add eggs one by one and keep beating.

Mix flours, baking powder, and salt and add to butter-egg mixture by spoonfuls. Mix until smooth batter forms.

Line a 9 x 9 inch / 23 x 23 centimeter pan with parchment paper and transfer batter to the pan. Top with raspberries.

Cut up cold butter and place in a medium mixing bowl with flour and sugar. Massage with your fingers until small curds form (similar in size to cottage cheese). Top raspberries with crumble topping. Bake for about 50–55 minutes, until golden brown on top.

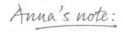

Anna's note:

If you like a thinner cake, bake in a larger pan (11 x 9 inches / 28 x 23 centimeters) but shorten the baking time to about 40–45 minutes.

Shortbread Cookies
– Ciastka kruche –

My grandma was the absolute best at making these cookies. These simple, crumbly shortbread cookies were always prepared around Christmas holidays. Every time I eat them, memory of her rushes to my heart.

Yields: *About 40 small cookies* **Prep time:** *10 minutes* **Cook time:** *1 hour*

2 c / 250 g of all-purpose flour
5 oz / 140 g of butter
3 egg yolks (reserve whites)
½ c / 60 g of powdered sugar
½ tsp of vanilla extract
¼ c / 60 ml of sour cream
2 tsp of baking powder
Pinch of salt

Place flour in a mixing bowl, add butter cut into small pieces and the rest of the ingredients. Gently mix with hands until just combined and form a dough ball. Don't work it too much, as it will make for a dense cookie.

When the mixture is combined, if you still see bits of butter, that's okay. Butter will melt while baking and make for a flaky cookie. Wrap the dough ball in plastic and refrigerate for an hour.

When ready, preheat oven to 350°F / 180°C, divide the ball into smaller portions and roll out onto a floured surface to about a ⅜–¼ inch / 4–5 millimeter thickness. Using your favorite cookie cutter, cut out shapes and place onto a baking sheet covered with parchment paper.

Slightly beat egg whites with a fork and, using a kitchen brush, brush each cookie with egg whites and sprinkle with a pinch of granulated sugar.

Bake for about 8–10 minutes, or until golden brown.

Sweet Cheese Rolls

— Drożdżówki z serem —

*Yeast rolls filled with a sweet mixture of farmer's cheese with raisins.
I love these delicious buns right as they come out of the oven.*

Yields: *16–18 rolls* **Prep time:** *20 minutes* **Cook time:** *2 hours*

— Dough —

2 ¼ tsp of active dry yeast or 40 g of fresh yeast

⅓ c / 65 g of granulated sugar

3 c / 375 g of all-purpose flour

1 c / 250 ml of milk

2 tbsp of melted butter

2 whole eggs

1 tsp of vanilla extract

Pinch of salt

Place yeast, 2 tablespoons of sugar, 4 tablespoons of flour and ½ cup of warm milk in a small mixing bowl and mix to combine. Cover with a clean kitchen towel and set aside to activate for 30 minutes in a warm spot.

In the meantime, melt butter and set aside to cool a bit.

When yeast mixture is ready, place the rest of the flour, sugar, eggs, milk, butter, vanilla, and salt in the mixing bowl of your stand mixer, add yeast mixture and, with the hook attachment, knead until a dough ball forms, plus additional 4–5 minutes. Dough should resemble pizza dough. If it's too loose, add a bit more flour.

When dough is ready, sprinkle with flour, cover with a kitchen towel and set aside to rise for about 1 hour in a warm spot. Dough should double in size.

Continued on the next page.

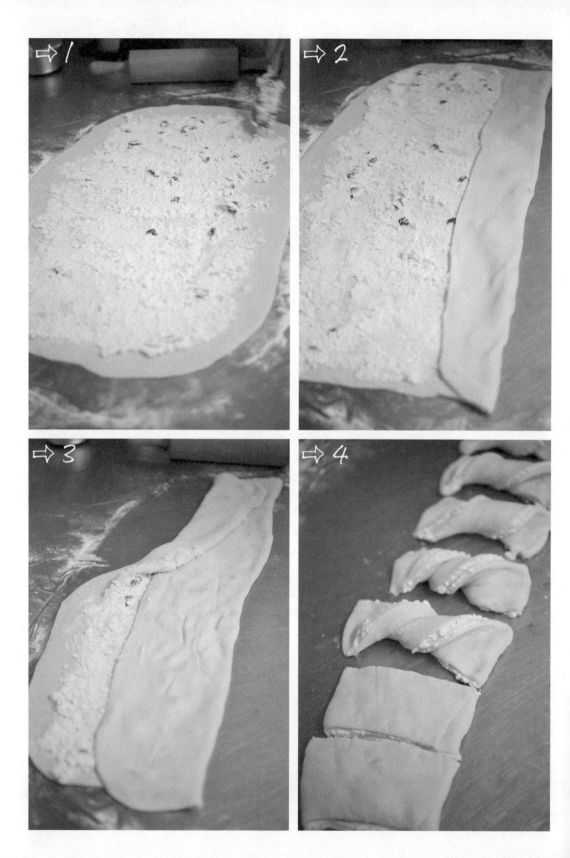

– Filling & Baking –

1 lb / 500 g of farmer's cheese*
2.5 tbsp of granulated sugar
2 egg yolks
¼ c of raisins

ADDITIONALLY:

1 egg
1–2 tbsp of sour cream

In the meantime, prepare filling by combining all ingredients. If your farmer's cheese seems too dry, add a tablespoon or two of sour cream. Break up farmer's cheese with a fork, add the rest of the ingredients and mix until well combined. Set aside.

When dough is ready, transfer onto a floured surface, knead a few times to help get the air out. Divide it in half. Roll out the first half into a rectangle. You want the dough to be pretty thin, about ⅛ inch / 3 millimeters thick (see photos).

Place half of the filling on the whole surface of the dough and fold the dough as shown in the photos on previous page.

With a sharp knife or a pizza cutter, cut into 7–8 even slices. Twist each slice once or twice.

Place rolls on a cookie sheet and brush with beaten egg. Set aside for at least 30 minutes to rise. Repeat the process with the other half of the dough and filling.

Preheat oven to 350°F / 180°C.

Place in hot oven and bake for about 15–18 minutes, until golden brown.

These sweet buns are also delicious when filled with poppyseed filling. Use recipe from page 253.

Anna's note:

* Substitute with cream cheese, if not available.

Yeast Babka with Raisins

— Babka drożdżowa z rodzynkami —

Extra soft yeast bundt cake with raisins, topped with sugar glaze is always prepared as part of the Easter celebrations.

Yields: *1 bundt cake*   **Prep time:** *1.5 hours*   **Cook time:** *50 minutes*

1.5 oz / 40 g fresh yeast or 0.7 oz / 20 g / 3.5 tsp of active dry yeast

¾ c / 175 ml warm milk

¾ c / 150 g of granulated sugar

4 c / 500 g of all-purpose flour

¾ c / 100 g of raisins

1 tbsp of corn starch

¼ c / 60 ml of water or favorite high-proof alcohol (rum, whiskey, brandy, etc.)

5 oz / 150 g of butter, melted and cooled

1 egg + 4 egg yolks

1 tsp of vanilla extract

Zest of half a lemon

Pinch of salt

Additional butter to grease pan

FROSTING:

1 c / 120 g of powdered sugar

A few drops of freshly squeezed lemon juice

5–6 tsp of hot water

Place yeast, warm milk, sugar, and ½ cup of flour in a mixing bowl and mix until dissolved. Cover and set aside for 15 minutes in a warm spot.

Place raisins in a small bowl, add water (or alcohol) and soak for 10 minutes. Melt butter and set aside to cool.

Place raisins in a strainer and add corn starch. Shake it around to cover raisins and get rid of excess corn starch.

*After 15 minutes of yeast mixture proofing, add raisins, remaining flour, butter, egg, egg yolks, vanilla extract, lemon zest, and salt and mix to form dough. Transfer onto a clean, floured surface and knead for **no less than** 15 minutes. Add another tablespoon of flour if dough is too wet.*

*Grease bundt pan with butter, place dough in pan, distribute evenly. Cover with a towel and set aside for at least 2 hours in a warm spot. The dough has to (at least) **DOUBLE** in size.*

Preheat oven to 350°F / 180°C. Place babka in the middle rack and bake for 40–45 minutes. When done, let rest for a few minutes and then transfer to a cooling rack.

To make icing, place powdered sugar in a small mixing bowl. Add a few drops of lemon juice and keep adding 1 teaspoon of hot water at a time. Mix until combined; it should create a paste. Adjust the amount of water and sugar for the desired thickness of the icing. Pour over cake once cake has cooled off.

Anna's note:

This cake is often made with raisins. For this recipe use ¾ cup / 100 g. Place raisins in a small bowl and add water (or alcohol—whiskey, brandy, rum—about ¼ cup / 60 ml).
Right before step 2, place raisins in a strainer and add corn starch (1 tablespoon). Shake it around to cover raisins and get rid of excess corn starch. Add to dough in step 2.
You can also top this sweet bread with your favorite fruit. We often add ripe plums, sour cherries or rhubarb. You can add those right before topping cake with crumble.

Yeast Cake with Crumble

—Placek drożdżowy z kruszonką—

Slightly sweet yeast bread covered in buttery crumble was always such a big treat in my home. The soft, cloud-like cake is absolutely irresistible and was always gone in no time.

Yields: *9 x 11 inch pan or 2 loaf pans* **Prep time:** *15 minutes* **Cook time:** *2 hours*

YEAST STARTER:

1.5 oz / 40 g fresh yeast or 0.7 oz / 3.5 tsp of active dry yeast

¾ c / 175 ml warm milk

¾ c / 150 g of granulated sugar

½ c / 60 g of all-purpose flour

DOUGH:

4 c / 500 g of all-purpose flour

5 oz / 150 g of butter, melted and cooled

1 egg + 4 egg yolks

1 tsp of vanilla extract

Pinch of salt

Additional butter to grease pan (or parchment paper)

CRUMBLE:

⅔ c / 80 g of all-purpose flour

⅓ c / 40 g of powdered sugar

2 oz / 55 g cold butter

Place yeast, warm milk and sugar and ½ cup of flour in a mixing bowl and mix until dissolved. Cover and set aside for 15 minutes in a warm spot in the kitchen. Melt butter and set aside to cool.

*After 15 minutes of yeast mixture proofing, add flour, butter, egg, egg yolks, vanilla extract, and salt and mix to form dough. Transfer onto a clean, floured surface and knead for **no less than** 10 minutes. Add another tablespoon of flour if dough is too wet.*

*Return dough to mixing bowl and let rise until it **doubles** in size!*

*Grease 9 x 11 inch / 23 x 28 centimeter pan (or two loaf pans) with butter (or line with parchment paper), place dough in pan, distribute evenly. Cover with a towel and set aside for another 30–60 minutes in a warm spot. The dough has to **DOUBLE** in size **again**!*

To make crumble, place all ingredients in a food processor and pulse until mixture looks like "dust" - only about 5–10 seconds. Move mixture to a mixing bowl and squeeze with your hands to create lumps.

Preheat oven to 350°F / 180°C. Cover top of dough with crumble. Bake for 30–35 minutes.

– Index –

SAUSAGE:

Beans & sausage, *109*
Blood sausage 3 ways, *115*
Cabbage & sausage soup, *7*
Fresh sausage, *127*
Hunter's stew, *131*
Smoked sausage, *143*
Sour rye soup, *45*
Toasted sandwiches, *148*

SOUR RYE:

Sour rye soup, *45*
Sour rye starter, *43*

SORREL:

Sorrel soup, *41*

TOMATO:

Beans & sausage, *109*
Cabbage & sausage soup, *7*
Fish & rice sandwich spread, *157*
Hunter's stew, *131*
Tomato sauce, *118*
Tomato soup, *47*
Tomato & onion salad, *225*

TRIPE:

Tripe soup, *49*

TURKEY:

Turkey steaks with horseradish cream
sauce, *147*

YEAST:

Donuts, *244*
Onion rolls, *200*
Poppyseed roll, *253*
Sauerkraut & mushroom pies, *221*
Sweet cheese rolls, *261*
Yeast apple pancakes, *103*
Yeast babka with raisins, *265*
Yeast cake with crumble, *267*

My family recipes: